THE

MORMONIZING

OF AMERICA

STEPHEN MANSFIELD

New York Times Best-selling Author

THE

MORMONIZING

OF AMERICA

HOW THE MORMON RELIGION BECAME A DOMINANT FORCE IN POLITICS, ENTERTAINMENT, AND POP CULTURE

WORTHY
PUBLISHING

Copyright © 2012 by Stephen Mansfield

Published by Worthy Books, an imprint of Worthy Publishing Group, a division of Worthy Media, Inc., One Franklin Park, 6100 Tower Circle, Suite 210, Franklin, TN 37067.

eBook available at www.worthypublishing.com

Audio distributed through Oasis Audio; visit www.oasisaudio.com

Library of Congress Control Number: 2012937694

For foreign and subsidiary rights, contact rights@worthypublishing.com.

ISBN: 978-1-617950-78-0 (hardcover)
ISBN: 978-1-68397-288-4 (trade paper)

Cover Design: Christopher Tobias, Tobias Design
Cover Photos: Composite angel, © Paul Chesley/Getty Images; Flag, © iStockphoto.com Interior
Typesetting: Susan Browne Design

Printed in the United States of America

To
David Foster
(1953–2012)

ALSO BY STEPHEN MANSFIELD

*Never Give In: The Extraordinary
Character of Winston Churchill*

*Then Darkness Fled: The Liberating
Wisdom of Booker T. Washington*

*Forgotten Founding Father: The Heroic
Legacy of George Whitefield*

The Faith of George W. Bush

The Faith of the American Soldier

Benedict XVI: His Life and Mission

The Faith of Barack Obama

The Search for God and Guinness

CONTENTS

Acknowledgments

I was five minutes into Dr. Grant Underwood's class at Brigham Young University when I made my strategic mistake. Grant had graciously invited me to participate in his Mormonism in the American Experience class and I had eagerly accepted. Once I arrived, he urged me to introduce myself to the students. That's when I nearly fell into the pond. I talked about my life for a while and then explained how my fascination with faith had brought me to them. Feeling the moment, I wanted to say something about how welcoming everyone had been, not just at BYU but at headquarters in Salt Lake City and everywhere I had spoken with LDS scholars, politicians, or believers around the country. That's when I used one of my favorite throwaway lines: "Will you adopt me?"

I say it all the time. If someone bakes something wonderful and offers me a bite, I'll say, "Oh, how nice. Will you adopt me?" If a friend builds a house with a beautiful view and a pool, I'll almost automatically ask, "Will you adopt me so I can live here?" So the words fell thoughtlessly from my lips—in that class at Brigham Young University . . . in front of supercharged young Latter-day Saints. There, you know, just south of Salt Lake City and the Temple and all.

The bright kid in the class—which is all of them, of course, but by bright I mean smart aleck—didn't miss a beat. He cleared his throat and said, "Well, of course, we will. Would you like for us to call the missionaries?"

And the whole class cracked up. They had me. Of course they would adopt me. That's what they're on earth to do. Family. Eternity. Belonging. Connection. Progressing together. Grant gave me a look that said, *Wow, you walked right into that one. And you have a doctorate? Must be in basket weaving or volleyball or something.*

It was the type of warm, human moment in which far more is radiated than anyone tries to describe. I loved it. It was sweet and endearing, and I saw in that instant a bit of the enveloping community that has enabled the Latter-day Saints to do what few religions have in the tumultuous modern world: allow people to belong before they believe.

I found this same openness and—what is it? Kindness? Or some mystical gift for connection?—as I plied Dr. Kathleen Flake of Vanderbilt University with what were probably insulting questions at a Nashville Starbucks. Onlookers must have wondered at our loud, fun, passionate interchanges about cults and speaking in tongues and how much "my kind" gets wrong about "her kind." She was amazing and I am grateful.

Equally impressive and gracious were the many learned souls who gave the gift of their time during my journeys through Utah. Historian Glen Leonard of the Latter Day Saints Church History Museum and the Mormon History Association spent unhurried hours with me and only then explained he would have to leave me because he had to get back to settling his mother's estate. He had interrupted his sad duty just to guide me. I was deeply moved. Michael Otterson, chief executive of LDS Public Relations, offered fascinating perspective not only about the challenges of managing the official face of Mormonism today but also about his life as a British convert to the Church. Dr. Paul Reeve of the University of Utah patiently answered my questions and only then brought up his offense with something I had written. He might well have refused to meet with me at all. He didn't, and this is testament to his character and grace. Dr. Boyd Peterson of Utah Valley University's Mormon Studies program won me with his engaging laughter and eager mind. Our hours together were a delight. April Williamsen of the spectacular LDS Church History Library also captured me with her pleasant manner, thorough knowledge of her field, and the hilarious cast of characters she introduced me to in the historical preservation department.

My conversations with LDS outliers stirred me beyond anything I could have expected. I laughed and learned with Mary Ellen Robertson, Dan Wotherspoon, and Stephen Carter of *Sunstone* magazine. Rocky Anderson, former mayor of Salt Lake City, reshaped my understanding of his city and his former faith and did so with such gentleness and insight that I did not fully realize what had happened until days later. Never will I forget my hours with the Mormon "fundamentalists," normally a code word for polygamists. Anne Wilde opened her home and her story to me, allowing me to tour a world foreign to any I have known. Other polygamists who prefer not to be mentioned here nevertheless know of my gratitude. I was so captured by their struggles that I found myself defending them to state official friends one evening. While I was mid-rant, one of them looked at me in mock horror and said, "Oh no, you've joined them! Does your wife know she has a sister wife somewhere out here just north of Provo?"

Scholars and thinkers around the country spoke with me patiently and helped me understand. Jan Shipps, the leading non-Mormon scholar of Mormonism, was fierce in manning her positions and I saw what it means to love a field of study with your life. David Campbell of Notre Dame via Harvard and BYU was tremendously insightful, as was my friend Mitch Horowitz, whose book on the occult in America is essential. The brilliant and much maligned D. Michael Quinn taught me well, though I confess to being distracted by the echo of his sufferings in his voice. Tricia Erickson helped me feel the ex-Mormons' fire. It has not left me.

Those who work with me know that I am notoriously bored with literary mysteries. It is the brooding jock side of my personality beating my inner, bespectacled scholar into submission. The study of LDS history involves a number of these did-Shakespeare-write-Shakespeare-type debates, so I was grateful for a number of patient guides. Arthur Vanick of Spalding Research Associates skillfully helped me understand his life's work, and the kind souls at The Neal Maxwell Institute for Religious Scholarship at Brigham Young University steered me even to resources they wished I would not read. I am thankful and, well, impressed.

In the category of scholars and thinkers, I must again mention the amazing students at Brigham Young University. When I think back on this project, whatever else happens, I will always recall the eager faces on that campus. They are the LDS's new generation, and I think they have a sense they are bridging from what has been to some new, more fruitful arrangement with non-Mormon culture. They narrated their world with the easygoing manner of an experienced tour guide acquainted with myth and ignorance.

During one of my days at BYU, I mindlessly ordered a Diet Coke in the faculty dining room. The student/waitress looked at me with a comforting smile and said, "Now, our Diet Coke, you know, it doesn't have any caffeine." "That's fine," I said with a shrug. "I just didn't want you to be disappointed," she assured. Now, she could have let that go, because no one knows with certainty whether they are drinking caffeine free when it comes to soft drinks, but she felt she had to take a stand for full disclosure. It was charming.

The same happened when I wandered through BYU's bookstore. Right in the middle of that book lover's paradise is a candy store as large as any you'll see at the mall or a major theme park. I turned to the student escorting me and said, "My goodness. What's the deal with this?" I mean, there were great mountains of bagged candy of the kind you get at the grocery store but then there were bins of freshly made praline this and walnut that, crème-filled somethings next to cherry-centered something else. I'm sure no other university has anything like it.

My student shadow said, "You've got to understand. We don't snort cocaine. We don't smoke. We don't drink alcohol. We don't even drink caffeine."

"Yeah?" I said expectantly.

"Well, M&Ms are our drug of choice!" he said happily. It was clearly a line he had used before, but he broke into such self-satisfied laughter that I had to join him. And there we stood, a member of the Mormon priesthood and a decidedly non-Mormon guest, laughing about what would have been painful to discuss not too many years ago. It is the gift of the new generation, and it taught me more than all the statistics and growth projections stuffed into my notes.

No one had me laughing, though, like Glenn Beck. He is an odd blend of patriot and introvert, activist and morose monk. The English essayist William Hazlitt once wrote that "man is the only animal that laughs and weeps: for he is the only animal that is struck by the difference between what things are and what they ought to be." This is the disparity that enflames Beck's soul, the chasm from which his humor springs. It was a privilege to learn from him and an honor to hear him tearfully talk about his faith.

My ever-vigilant assistant, Emily Mulloy Prather, dug for treasure and scheduled interviews with skill while her home was racked with severe sickness not once but twice. She bore my unending demands with the patience of an angel and unearthed riches I could not have imagined. I found myself muttering gratitude for her Vanderbilt MBA, for her tenacious nature, and for the day she walked through our door those years ago.

It was pleasant to involve my college roommate, David Toberty, in this project. He advised me on a number of matters and, as usual, impressed me. Ten minutes into one of our conversations I saw again why he is a successful Los Angeles attorney. His keen mind, pleasant manner, and teacher's gift have been finely honed. I realize how far we have both come since we first shared dreams over midnight pizza those many years ago. His friendship honors me.

Jennifer Cooke sat with me at BrickTop's in Nashville and told me of her life on the edge of the Latter-day Saints. She had me laughing at her plans to marry Donny Osmond, marveling at the sweetness of her high school LDS friendships, yet grieving with her over the agonizing distance from those friends she endures today. Her memories touched me deeply, as did her love for those with whom she intensely disagrees.

As always, Chartwell Literary Group proved invaluable. Their skill with a manuscript, managing everything from photo rights to the editing process, and their ability to finesse an author in the direction he ought to go has again made Chartwell the literary ally I most need. I'm grateful beyond words.

It is now conventional wisdom that publishers roam their halls mumbling, "The only good author is a dead author" and authors sit at their desks thinking publishers have been sent to rid the earth of fine literature. This has not been my sentiment as I have worked with Worthy Publishing. I initially took my enjoyment of each of the Worthy staff as evidence of a likely curse. If I like them, I thought, it cannot go well. It has. I'm grateful for the professional relationship and for the investment of their care and skill.

There was a playlist for the writing of this album and it included "Cult of Personality" by Living Color, "Carry on Wayward Son" by Kansas, "All Things Shall Pass" by George Harrison, "Gimme Shelter" by Ashley Cleveland via the Rolling Stones, and any reel by the Tannahill Weavers just to blow the soot out of my mind. When one of my best friends died the week before this book was done, Vince Gill's "Go Rest High on That Mountain" drew out the grief.

In writing as in every other arena of life, my wife, Beverly, is more than muse, more than *paraclete* and guide. She transforms all I do with her wise, lovingly impatient, sometimes rowdy ways. When I think of her, and feel again the tender privilege of having her in my life, that line from Glen Campbell's "Wichita Lineman"—"And I need you more than want you. And I want you for all time"—comes to mind. My Mormon friends urged me to join with Bev for eternity. They were trying to help. "That is in God's hands," I said, thanking them. "Just to be in time with her is more than I deserve."

On Saintly Language

Like most religions, particularly religions with painful histories of persecution, the Church of Jesus Christ of Latter-day Saints is picky about what people call them. They prefer "The Church of Jesus Christ of Latter-day Saints." This, of course, becomes wearisome when it appears as often as it must in a full-length book about, you know, the Church of Jesus Christ of Latter-day Saints. This paragraph proves the point.

The solution seems to be the initials "LDS"—which stand, of course, for "Latter-day Saints." Nearly everyone in Salt Lake City uses this shorthand. "Are you LDS?" two people might ask each other. "He's the LDS lawyer" is another popular usage. There is even much love—and gratitude—for the phrase "LDS Church," and the faithful will use this phrase with satisfaction as well.

What apparently causes heartache is the phrase "Mormon Church." The word "Mormon" is considered a nickname for the faith and not a happy one for some reason. Members of the LDS will use the word "Mormon" but will never say "Mormon Church." You can say "Mormon Tabernacle Choir" and the "Book of Mormon" (the book, not the play), but you should not say "Mormon Church" because it is too informal and can signal that the LDS Church is built on a man who lived centuries ago. It isn't.

The other issue is that the Church of Jesus Christ of Latter-day Saints always capitalizes the word "Church" when referring to itself. In Salt Lake City, where most everyone you meet is LDS, it is standard when speaking to just say "the Church" to refer to everything Mormon—"the Church's teaching," "the Church's property," or "the Church is listening." Sometimes this is done with a nod of the head toward Temple Square, so it is wise to stay oriented when in Salt Lake City. If the word "Church" is ever written by a Mormon when referring to the LDS Church, it is always capitalized. It is *the* Church and a capital 'C' reminds us all. Any other church is designated with a pitifully small 'c.' So a member of the LDS will write, "John goes to First Baptist Church," thus writing the name properly. But if he should write, "John's church is weird," a small 'c' is used. If this same LDS member writes, "Our Church is awesome," it gets the Big C treatment.

Another surprisingly important matter: standard usage is to employ the phrase "Latter-day Saints" to refer to the LDS Church today, but to use its nonhyphenated version—"Latter Day Saints"—to refer to the faithful when Joseph Smith walked the earth. So the sentence "The Latter Day Saints marched to Nauvoo in 1840" would get the nonhyphenated treatment. The sentence "Ten Latter-day Saints went to see the play *The Book of Mormon*," would get the hyphenated treatment—and would not, by the way, be widely believed.

In this book, we will respect the convention of the hyphenated and nonhyphenated versions of the religion's name: no hyphen for the faithful who lived when Joseph Smith breathed; hyphen for every more recent Saint. It is standard usage now.

We will also observe the Church's preference for capitalizing the word *Church* when referring to the LDS Church. This is not because the author shares the LDS's regard for itself. It is simply an act of graciousness that has the added benefit of making it easier to distinguish which church (Church) is being referred to in the text.

This is where our literary largesse ends, though. In this book, *Mormons, LDS, Saints,* or *Church* are nearly interchangeable terms. The view in these chapters is that the word *Mormon* has lost whatever insult factor it may have had and has entered modern usage with no more venom than attached to the words *Anglican* or *Buddhist*—though with a good deal less than is attached to *Muslim* and slightly more than evoked by *Pentecostal*. The word *Mormon* also does not evoke the memory of a man for most moderns. Instead, it is simply a literary symbol for what is: the Church of Jesus Christ of Latter-day Saints and the grand sum of its proud accomplishments. Without malice we shall speak of the Mormon Church, use the term *Mormonism* to describe anything in the LDS world, and summon the word *Saints* with thought for no more than simply providing variety of expression.

One final matter. The author of this book is not a Mormon, and this book is intended neither to defend nor to prosecute Mormonism. It is meant to be an exploration of LDS influence in America, reaching into LDS Church history for origins and meaning. Still, positions will be taken. Controversies will be aired. Tensions will be defined.

During this process, nothing would make it more tedious than for nearly every sentence to be larded with "supposedly" or "allegedly" or "so says them." Therefore, if telling LDS history requires describing an angel showing up in Joseph Smith's bedroom one night—and it does—then the narrative here might read "Smith reported a visitation" or even "and a visitation came." It will almost certainly include the words, "And Moroni said . . ." The reader must always keep in mind that the author is portraying a religion not his own and is doing so with respect for both the Mormon people and good writing.

Thousands of disclaimers, however brief, do not a smooth read make. Similarly, a book about a people that takes every pain to refer to that people and their beliefs with derision need not have been written. It would indicate flawed scholarship, flawed literature, and flawed humanity. Best to simply state what Mormons believe, having first established that it is not the view of the author.

And now we have done so.

SCENES FROM THE LAND OF THE SAINTS

No question the Church of Jesus Christ of Latter-day Saints is "having a moment."[1]

—Newsweek

It is another day in the life of Mormon America.

For some news commentators, it is the next phase of an unfolding "Mormon Moment." For more than a few scholars, it is the latest stage in the surprising but assured Mormon ascent in our time. For large numbers of Christian evangelicals, it is the unfolding of a carefully crafted Mormon plan to rule the world from America. For the nation's Mormons, it is opportunity to face the tests that mean eternal progress beyond this "lone and dreary world." And for secular America, it is yet another occasion for the passing parade of oddities that Mormons have long supplied.

It is 9 a.m. in Utah. On the second floor of the Joseph Smith Memorial Building in Salt Lake City, Michael Otterson, head of Mormon public relations, sits in his corner office and tries to hide his weariness as he defends the spiritual fortress of the Latter-day Saints. He is in his late fifties; tall, distinguished, and smooth of manner—his British accent lending precision and weight to his every sentence. It is not hard to imagine him the newspaper editor he was for more than a decade before he made the move to Temple Square.

"No, I've not seen *The Book of Mormon* on Broadway," he says evenly to an interviewer. "Mormons don't go to R-rated movies or lewd plays. I have read the script, though, and I find it pretty blasphemous. Still, it hasn't hurt us."

"Hasn't hurt you?" the other man asks, his fingers capturing every word on the iPad in his lap. "How can that be? It is a biting deconstruction of everything Mormon. Haven't you heard Bill Maher sing its praises on HBO?"

"Yes. Of course, though Bill Maher is no one I take seriously. But I have read the reviews and there is something sweet about how the play is being perceived. You know, in the end, the missionaries win. Most of the reviews talk about this. And I can tell you that the musical is only driving interest in us. We've had our missionaries stopped on the streets of New York by people with questions about our faith. Local hotels have run out of the Book of Mormon and we've had to resupply them by the boxful."

"But it has to hurt you ultimately, doesn't it?" the writer presses, almost sympathetically. "It's a complete attack on everything you believe."

"Listen. Mormons have always been treated harshly. We are the only religion in the United States ever to be put under an extermination order. That was in Missouri. And the order was only rescinded fifteen years ago. We've been gunned down, imprisoned for our beliefs, and we've had our property confiscated again and again. We are certainly going to survive a spiteful Broadway play!"[2]

Thirty minutes' drive south of Salt Lake City, Anne Wilde sits at her kitchen table with an inquisitive researcher. It is late morning on an icy day and her low-roofed ranch house is warm and welcoming, the view of the Wasatch Mountains through her front picture window an inspiration.

Anne is in her early seventies with a stern face easy to envision on a Mormon pioneer's wife a century and a half ago. Yet there is kindness in her eyes and more than a hint of the suffering she has endured, of the hard path she has chosen.

"I was raised in the Latter-day Saints," she says quietly but proudly. "My second cousin was President Ezra Taft Benson, the leader of the LDS in the late 1980s and early '90s. I graduated with honors from Brigham Young University and married in the Temple. But then my marriage ended in divorce, and that's when I began studying the doctrines taught in the early Church. It became clear to me. The Prophet Joseph Smith taught that plural marriage is essential for celestial exaltation.

It still is, I believe. When President Woodruff banned plural marriage in 1890, it was a political move. It was a compromise. There was no 'thus saith the Lord.' And I haven't heard a 'thus saith the Lord' from the Church since."

"So how long were you a polyga—I mean, in a plural marriage, Anne?" the researcher asks.

"Thirty-three years. My husband's name was Ogden Kraut and I loved him with all my heart. He absolved my first marriage and then we were sealed. He had other wives and they lived in other homes. I only had one day of jealousy my whole life with him. We were very happy. We produced sixty-five books together, all helping to restore the original doctrines of the Church, plural marriage in particular. Ogden and I were very close. We had something very special."

Her guest is quiet for a moment. The two sit silently, thinking about the life Anne has led. Then he asks, "How did your family take your marriage to a man with other wives?"

"My parents never knew. It would have been too much for them. My neighbors didn't know either. And my children did not take it well. They never felt close to Ogden, never liked the kind of marriage it was. It has left us distant ever since."

"And are you close to Ogden's other wives now that he is dead?" the young man asks.

"They are all dead too. It is actually quite lonely for me now. In fact, even when they were living it was a bit lonely because they were all so much older and we lived in separate homes."

"So, Anne, you believe that you will be married to Ogden again in the next life, right? You trust that Ogden and all of his wives will live together for all eternity?"

"Yes. If I'm found worthy, I'll be with Ogden again in eternity and we will be like Heavenly Father. That's what I'm living for. I miss him. But please don't misunderstand: I loved Ogden, but I chose plural marriage because it's the price of celestial exaltation, the highest state in eternity. It's what the Prophet Joseph Smith taught. And I can tell you that it isn't easy to live, but it is the price of being saved at the highest level."

Fourteen hundred miles to the east, two Vanderbilt University football players stand in line at San Antonio Taco Company, the popular Mexican food joint just across 21st Avenue from the main campus. The place is known around town as SATCO and it has, no doubt, the best soft tacos in Nashville. The athletes, both pushing 250 pounds, plan to down a dozen of them each for lunch and they are loudly "talkin' smack" about whose turn it is to buy.

Suddenly, the taller one stops. His jaw drops open and he nods toward the door. Soon both are staring in awe.

The girl they can't look away from is a stunner. She has a full mane of billowing blond hair, the kind of body most men dream of, and the elegance of a dancer.

The two football players begin elbowing each other wordlessly. Each intends to be the first to approach.

Then the girl turns from the order counter in their direction. And they see what they couldn't before. Stretched across her chest are the words printed on her T-shirt: "I can't. I'm Mormon."

The two linemen stop shoving. Muffled laughter sounds from the lunchtime crowd. More than a few have been watching. And from behind the two comes the voice of another football player who has just arrived.

"Dee-niiiieed," he says, in the mock manner of an overexcited sportscaster.

It is 1300 hours Romeo and at a secure conference room at USCENTCOM, Lieutenant General Marshall Hollings is unhappy. "Major, I told you to bring me the right man for a snake-eater assignment and you bring me the Boy Scout we just met. And he's a Mormon? I need someone hard-boiled, Major. I don't need some fresh-faced ring knocker."

"Sir, I understand, but Captain Jensen is—"

"I know! I know! He's Annapolis and a SEAL Assault Team leader and he was decorated for Fallujah. And one of the Chiefs wants to marry him. I get it. But I need someone nasty, not a résumé. Do I have to spell it out?

"No, sir, but . . ."

"And a Mormon? I know it ain't PC, but you think a missionary can do this one?"

"Yes, sir. I understand, but please listen, sir. Jensen got that medal at Fallujah for the Carter Rescue and you remember that one. It got hand-to-hand. It was Jensen who snapped two of those insurgents and then he tied off Carter's artery bare-handed and under fire. He's no dilettante. And as for being Mormon, I know what you mean, sir. It ain't my cup of tea either. But it means he doesn't get high, doesn't smoke, doesn't drink, and doesn't chase skirts. He thinks his commission is straight from God. Since one of our other teams got fouled up because the leader was still toasted after a fight with his wife, I'm thinkin' this may be a change in the right direction. I also checked with Chaplain Schneider and there's nothing about being a Mormon that would keep Jensen from doing a hit on a holy—"

"Got it! Enough. I'll go with your rec, Major."

"I don't think you'll be disappointed, sir."

"It's not my disappointment I'm thinkin' about, Major. It's the lives in this one man's hands. Get Jensen back here. And call JAG."

"Yes, sir."

"A Mormon? The best man for *this*? Well, all right then. Let's get it done."

David Green opens the door of his room at Columbia's John Jay dorm and sees his roommate sitting at his desk, MacBook Pro in front of him, head buried in his hands. He's close to tears.

"T-man! What's wrong?"

Silence. And then, sadly, "G, I feel so stupid. I bought all this junk for so many years. My whole family did. But they didn't tell us the whole thing, man. Why would they hide this stuff?"

"Uh, T-Man. Slow it down. What are you talking about?"

"I got an e-mail from my sister today."

"She's okay?"

"Yeah. Except she's attending UVA and, you know, that's the South. They can be pretty fundy down there, so she's had some people messing with her about the Church. Well, someone got in her face and started dumping a bunch of stuff about our history on her. You know how it goes: they told her she'd be a coward if she didn't check out what they said for herself. Most of it was that Baptist anti-Mormon *shtick*."

"Okay, well, did she?"

"She did."

"Yeah?"

"And . . . she's decided they were right. Now she's all confused. And I have to tell you, G, so am I. Given some of the links she's sent me, I'm not sure what to believe."

"T-man!"

"Yeah, and you can't imagine how humiliating this is after all the years I spent in LDS schools. They just didn't tell us."

"Tell you what? I mean, how could those fundy nitwits say anything new?"

"For one thing, they said that Mormons massacred over a hundred people at Mountain Meadows—"

"Well, you knew that. We saw the movie. But that was like a hundred and fifty years ago!"

"Yeah, but they didn't tell us how the Church covered it all up. I mean, this was like the LDS Watergate. Listen, in our institute history class, they got through this whole Mountain Meadows thing in about two pages. You can't believe how they skipped over it. But, dude, they did not tell the truth about how that wagon train of people died. Those folks raised a white flag and gave up all their weapons. That's when the Saints acted like they were going to help and then shot everybody. And they got Indians to kill the women and children while the whites killed the men. Imagine what that was like."

"Unbelievable! Did they make anyone pay for this?"

"Yeah. Guess who? Brigham Young's son! Well, adopted son anyway. And do you think the Prophet Young didn't know what his son was doing? Guess what Brigham Young said when they put up a memorial a few years later? You know that scripture that says, 'Vengeance is mine and I will repay, saith the Lord'? Young said, 'Vengeance is mine and I have taken a little.'"

"Hey, T-Man. I know this is a bummer. But lighten up. I mean, does it make that much difference?"

"Yeah. It does. You don't understand, G. Our president is a prophet. He's a seer. We don't think of him like you do your Rabbi Hahn. He's . . . you know . . . a man who hears from Heavenly Father directly. Like open heaven kind of stuff. They can't tell us that and then lie about all this history."

It is 3:55 p.m. in Dallas. Ryan Dalbert is exiting North Stemmons Freeway as Presbyterian Hospital comes into view. He might just be on time. He has spent his last ounce of grace teaching the circulatory system to sophomores and doesn't need the stress of being late. He pulls into the hospital parking lot, gratefully finds a space up front and parks. As he does, he sees Jim Beals coming from his car. This fills him with relief. Jim is an older man who has done this many times before.

"Jim, I'm glad you're here. Sorry you have to be, though."

"Elder," Beals greets Dalbert, nodding with a smile.

At first Dalbert thinks Beals is a bit formal. They are friends, after all. But when he turns his head back toward the hospital, he sees why the older man was brief. Young Miguel Padilla's family is already approaching.

Dalbert understands almost nothing of what happens next. He's just moved to the metroplex from St. Paul and doesn't speak a word of Spanish. Elder Beals has lived in Texas all his life and his Spanish is passable. Dalbert is grateful: he thought he was going to have to do this one on his own.

The seven walk together into the hospital and find Miguel's room. The eerie rhythm of the respirator spills out into the hall and Mrs. Padilla begins to cry. When they enter the room, Beals gestures for the family to sit on the two short couches. Dalbert and Beals then look at Miguel. There is no change. Since the Friday night he snapped his neck in the game against Permian, he has not responded—not even to his mother's voice.

The room is filled with flowers, signed footballs, and brightly decorated posters. The two elders would like to look it all over, but they know what they have to do. They each move to opposite sides of Miguel's bed. Elder Beals prays silently for a moment and then pulls his key ring from his pocket, finds the little vial, and opens the lid. It is a vial of oil—Dalbert knows this oil is pure olive oil consecrated in advance for just such a moment. Beals dribbles a few drops of the oil onto Miguel's bandaged forehead and then gestures to Dalbert. Beals wants him to give the blessing. Now Dalbert feels a bit guilty. He had hoped when he heard that Elder Beals would be with him that the older man would give the priesthood blessing. It's been a busy day.

Mrs. Padilla is so touched that two Elders are praying for her son that she leans into her husband and begins to weep. Whatever happens to her sweet Miguel, she is thankful to be in the Church, to be part of a people who have the restored priesthood and who believe that miracles happen in this life.

The priesthood blessing begins. Both men lay their hands gently on Miguel and Dalbert starts to pray out loud. He mentions the priesthood restored to Joseph Smith and then passed down, speaks of the power in the "true and living Church," and then commands healing to come into Miguel's body and life.

The two men are still praying silent final prayers when they hear one of the little boys behind them say, "*Dios mio! Anda!*"

The Elders turn their heads to the child and then back to the bed between them. They see, then, what the child has seen.

Miguel has just opened his eyes.

"The petition is denied by unanimous vote of the members. Thank you, gentlemen. There being no further business, the Salt Lake City Planning and Zoning Commission is adjourned. Good afternoon. "

The gavel sounds. The commission and its attending petitioners, lawyers, engineers, and city planners disband. There is hint of an evening snow in the sky and the roads are likely to be jammed. The room empties in seconds.

Almost. Mike Stacey does not move. He sits hunched over on the second row, slowly shaking his head. He cannot believe what has just happened.

"I told you, Mike." The voice belongs to Darryl Moss. He's irritated, having just fought against the flow of bodies to get to the chair next to Mike. He's also irritated by the farce that has just occurred in the room. "We should never have tried to put this thing anywhere near LDS land."

"Ugh. I need a drink. These guys didn't even try to hide it. They just aren't going to let a wine and cigar bar anywhere near their holy ground. Even near their city!"

"No. And they'll fight you most anywhere in the state."

"I guess I'm gonna have to appeal."

"Appeal! To whom? To what? They got this whole state locked up. Who you goin' to appeal to?"

"All right. All right. Calm down."

"I'm askin'! The city council is mainly LDS. The state legislature is 70 percent LDS. The stinkin' governor is LDS. And even the Supreme Court—let's see, yeah, four out of the five of them are LDS too! It's a Mormon Taliban around here. Only the mayor's got any guts, and they've got him surrounded."

"Man, we're in trouble. What are we going to do?"

"Well, I had breakfast with Rocky Anderson this morning. You know, my buddy who was the mayor once? Oh, he told me a few things you might do. Let's see. Salt Lake City has the largest number of porn subscribers in the nation. You could go home and watch some porn. Or you could go have sex in the woods. We got the highest rate of arrest for that kind of thing of any city in America. And therefore we got the fastest climbing rate of chlamydia and a whole host of other sexually transmitted diseases. So, you could sit around and think about that. Oh, and then there's always Prozac—good old Vitamin

P—and we use more of that per person than any other city. You could just enjoy being high."

"You're not helping me, Darryl," Stacey says mournfully.

"I'm not trying to help you. I'm trying to get you to listen to sense and take this thing to another city. Heck, we were goin' to have to have a 'Zion Wall' anyway. A Zion Wall! Can you believe it? We were going to have to spend our good money to build a wall so the Saints wouldn't have to see folks drink—in a wine and cigar bar, for heaven's sake!"

"Doesn't matter now."

"You're absolutely right. It doesn't. We should have done this in Vegas like I said. A Zion Wall? This state's a loony bin."

Jed and Michele Oderson hold hands and speak tenderly to each other across the glass-topped table in their Chantilly, Virginia, kitchen. It is late in the evening and their nine children are either upstairs in bed asleep or studying with the headphones blaring. It is a good moment to talk.

Jed came home early from his work at Northrop Grumman to push the kids along and add a father's firmness to the evening's instructions. It was all to safeguard this moment, this all-important discussion. Now, the time has finally come.

"Are you sure, my love? It is not the money I'm concerned about. Heavenly Father will provide. But we shouldn't be foolish."

"What else can I do, Jed? We are incomplete. There are more of us yet to come."

"How can we be sure? And even if we were certain, surely your health absolves us."

"It is our duty, honey. I know you believe as I do that our family has already existed in premortality. I've become absolutely certain there are still more spirits who are part of us. It is a mother's job to know. We need to conceive so that the spirits of our unborn children can assume their bodies and be with us for time and all eternity."

"Spirits? Children? You're talking about more than one."

"Yes. I believe we have three more children waiting to be with us."

"But, honey, the last time you nearly didn't make it. Remember that placenta previa crisis? We almost lost Spencer. And you! How can we do this?"

"You remember what Patriarch James said when he laid his hands on me and gave me the blessing. He saw what was before. He saw our number in premortality. We have to act on what we know, on the word of prophecy."

"So there are twelve," Jed said quietly. He thought of what the guys at work would say about so many children. It would be crude, certainly. He would never tell Michele. But the thought of it made him smile slyly—for a moment.

"So you are certain?" he asked her, looking into the eyes he had loved so many years.

"Yes, babe. We have to do this."

"Okay. All right. I get it. I'll call the bishop tomorrow and ask him to walk with us in this. It's a huge test. We'll need him.

"We've made the right choice, Jed."

Across the country, at Orange County Destiny Church, Pastor Jeffrey Wills is teaching the next evening class in his four-month series on cults and world religions. The topic tonight is "The Mormon Menace." Just over 150 have turned out and are now scattered throughout the sanctuary, notebooks in hand. They are eager to learn. Pastor Wills is a gifted teacher, a man known for being well read and a graduate of some of the best evangelical schools in the country: Wheaton, Trinity, and Fuller Theological Seminary.

Wielding an infrared clicker to advance his PowerPoint slides, Wills nears his closing thoughts. "I suppose the best way to express this is to say that Joseph Smith had a reputation as a diviner and a treasure seeker in his hometown in upstate New York. Then, when he started claiming that an angel named Moroni—an angel who was actually a man who had lived 1,400 years before!—appeared to him and told him about a book on gold plates buried nearby in a hill, he translated those plates using 'seer stones.' This was an occult practice in which men saw messages in magical stones. Much of the Book of Mormon was 'translated' by Joseph Smith while he looked through seer stones at the bottom of his hat."

"Once Smith gathered followers he started having revelations that served his personal agenda. He even had some revelations that rebuked his wife for not being excited about the practice of polygamy. Listen to this. This is in what the Mormons call their *Doctrines and Covenants*, one of their holy books. I'm reading from section 132, verses 54 and 55:

'And I command mine handmaid, Emma Smith, to abide and cleave unto my servant Joseph, and to none else. But if she will not abide this commandment she shall be destroyed, saith the Lord; for I am the Lord thy God, and will destroy her if she abide not in my law.'

"Apparently, Smith's wife wasn't too keen about her husband marrying other women. So he had a revelation to convince her. Trust me, I wouldn't try that at home with Jen!"

The room erupts in knowing laughter. The pause allows one of the church's deacons to ask a question.

"So, Pastor, what is the truth about the Book of Mormon? Should we see it as a human fabrication by Joseph Smith or do you think it was dictated by some spiritual force?"

"Great question. I think the Book of Mormon is Joseph Smith's vain imaginings combined with what the apostle Paul called 'doctrines of demons.' And given the influence Mormons are gaining in this country, it may be the most destructive book on earth."

"One last thought, guys, and then I'll let you go. In the Satanic Bible, written by Anton Szandor LaVey, there is a list of the names for Satan. You know what one of them is? It is 'Mormo.' Here, I've put it on a slide. Be sure to write this down. It's from the Greek name for 'King of the Ghouls.' It's on page fifty-nine of the paperback version. Friends, I think this tells us all we need to know about what Mormonism really is.

"Okay. It's late. I'll let you go. Remember to pray for the Mormons. Good night!"

"Listen, I'm telling you. It ain't the dang doctrines!"

J. W. Woodlow says this last word so it rhymes with "vines." He's worked up. He doesn't care much for religion, but he isn't going to let that fool John McManus tell him his son has done wrong. The other night-shift workers in the lumber mill break room are all tuned in. Maybe there'll be a fight. Sometimes there are some during these 11:30 p.m. breaks, when men are tired and tempers flare.

"I asked my next-door neighbor. He's been a Mormon his whole life. Said he saw that same list in *USA Today* and just rolled his eyes. Said there weren't but two or three things in all them ten beliefs he even cared about. It's the community, he said. The community! That's the thing! My boy just wants to be in a church that cares about folks if he's going to start a family."

"What your boy wants has something to do with blue eyes and the best cook in Alabama," McManus shoots back evenly. "He'd become a durn Muslim if that's what she wanted. And I'm telling you, he's getting himself mixed up in a cult and you're going be sorry."

J. W.'s face reddens. He can feel his anger coming up and he knows he can't let it rise all the way. He's been here before.

"Listen, I wouldn't give you that empty cup right there for pretty much any religion. But let me tell you what. If I was shopping for a religion just for what it did for my family even if I knew it wasn't true, I'd choose the Mormons any day."

"You're nuts! A bunch of angel worshipers?"

Woodlow ignores this stupidity. McManus, the idiot Catholic, thinks Mormons worship angels because he's seen the Temple in Birmingham and it has a statue of an angel on top.

Holding up his fingers to number his arguments, Woodlow plows on. "They're a moral people. They don't even drink Diet Coke, for Pete's sake. They got huge families and they hang on to them tight because they think they're going to be together in eternity. They got churches that're run better than this mill. They set things back in their Bishop's Storehouse so they could survive a nuclear attack if they had to. They teach their kids well and then they send 'em to the best schools for college. They even make the family sit together every week. While you're watchin' your Falcons get whipped on a Monday night they're talking about God and playing with their kids. My neighbor says Mormons live longer, make more money, have less divorce, and have more influence in society than any other religion. Talk about influence: you're going to have one in the White House one day. Now, let's see: your Father George was doing all right on that whole influence thing until—oh yeah! That's right!—he got shipped to oblivion because he—"

The whistle sounds, signaling the end of the break. Woodlow, feeling the moment, stands up, shoots his chair back with his knees and leans across the table toward McManus.

"Yeah, I think my son's made a pretty good choice." He drills McManus with his blue-gray eyes and then storms out into the night.

These, then, are scenes from a day in Mormon America. They each actually occurred, they each reveal a facet of the faith or its opposition, and they each depict thinking that is part of the "Mormon Moment" of our time. The future of Mormonism and its influence upon our age will be determined by how episodes such as these and a million others like them play out in the years to come. They will occur at kitchen tables and in offices, on military bases and on the grounds of corporations, in television studios and even in our nation's corridors of power.

Mormonism has arrived, in a sense, but it has not just arrived at a moment of prominence. It has also arrived at a crucible, perhaps even at a crisis, that will determine all that comes after for the Saints. This too is the meaning of the

"Mormon Moment." It is a grand, uniquely American saga that must be understood in order to fully comprehend our age—a period some have called "the great age of the Latter-day Saints."

ENGINE OF THE MORMON ASCENT

It is almost impossible to write fiction about the Mormons, for the reason that Mormon institutions and Mormon society are so peculiar that they call for constant explanation.[1]

—Wallace Stegner, *Mormon Country*

There are nearly seven million Mormons in America. This is the number the Mormons themselves use.[2] It's not huge. Seven million is barely 2 percent of the country's population. It is the number of people who subscribe to *Better Homes and Gardens* magazine. London boasts seven million people. So does San Francisco. It's a million more people than live in the state of Washington; a million less than in the state of Virginia. It's so few, it's the same number as were watching the January 24, 2012, Republican debate.

In fact, worldwide, there are only about fourteen million Mormons. That's fourteen million among a global population just reaching *seven billion*. Fourteen million is the population of Cairo or Mali or Guatemala. It's approximately the number of people who tune in for the latest hit show on network television every week. Fourteen million Americans ate Thanksgiving dinner in a restaurant in 2011. That's how few fourteen million is.

Yet in the first decade or so of the new millennium, some members of the American media discovered the Mormons and began covering them as though the Latter-day Saints had just landed from Mars. It was as though Utah was about to invade the rest of the country. It was all because of politics and pop culture, of course. Mitt Romney and John Huntsman were in pursuit of the White House. Glenn Beck was among the nation's most controversial news commentators. Stephenie Meyer had written the astonishingly popular Twilight series about vampires. Matt Stone and Trey Parker had created the edgy *South Park* cartoon series—which included a much-discussed episode about Mormons—and then went on to create the blatantly blasphemous and Saint-bashing Broadway play *The Book of Mormon*. It has become one of the most successful productions in American theater history.

Meanwhile, more than a dozen Mormons sat in the US Congress, among them Harry Reid, the Senate Majority Leader. Mormons led JetBlue, American Express, Marriott, Novell, Deloitte and Touche, Diebold, and Eastman Kodak. Management guru Stephen Covey made millions telling them how to lead even better. There were Mormons commanding battalions of US troops and Mormons running major US universities. There were so many famous Mormons, in fact, that huge websites were launched just to keep up with it all. Notables ranged from movie stars like Katherine Heigl to professional athletes to country music stars like Gary Allan to reality television contestants and even to serial killers like Glenn Helzer, whose attorney argued that the Saints made him the monster he was. The media graciously reminded the public that Mormon criminals were nothing new, though: Butch Cassidy of *Butch Cassidy and the Sundance Kid* fame was also a Mormon, they reported.

Most media coverage treated this "Mormon Moment" as though it was just that: the surprising and unrelated appearance of dozens of Mormons on the national stage—for a moment. More than a few commentators predicted it would all pass quickly. This new Mormon visibility would lead to new scrutiny, they said, and once the nation got reacquainted with tales of "holy underwear" and multiple wives and Jewish Indians and demonized African Americans and a book printed on gold plates buried in upstate New York, it would all go quiet again and stay that way for a generation. In the meantime, reruns of HBO's *Big Love* and The Learning Channel's *Sister Wives* would make sure Mormon themes didn't die out completely.

What most commentators did not understand was that their "Mormon Moment" was more than a moment, more than an accident, and more than a matter of pop culture and fame alone. The reality was—and is—that the Church of Jesus Christ of Latter-day Saints has reached critical mass. It is not simply that a startling number of Mormons have found their way onto America's flat-screen TVs and so brought visibility to their religion. It is that the Church of Jesus Christ of Latter-day Saints has reached sufficient numbers—and has so permeated every level of American society on the strength of its religious value—that prominent politicians, authors, athletes, actors, newscasters, and even murderers are the natural result, in some cases even the intended result. Visible, influential Mormons aren't outliers or exceptions. They are fruit of the organic growth of their religion.

The Mormon Rise

In 1950, there were just over a million Mormons in the world. Most of these were located in the Intermountain West of the United States, a region of almost lunar landscape between the Rocky Mountains to the East and the Cascades and Sierra Nevada Mountains to the West. The religion was still thought of as odd by most Americans. There had been famous Mormons like the occasional US Senator or war hero, but these were few and far between. There had even been a 1940 Hollywood movie entitled *Brigham Young* that told the story of the Saints' mid-1800s trek from Illinois to the region of the Great Salt Lake. Its producers worked hard to strain out nearly every possible religious theme, a nod to the increasingly secular American public. Though it starred heavyweights like Vincent Price and Tyrone Power, the movie failed miserably, even in Utah. Especially in Utah.

Then, in 1951, a man named David O. McKay became the "First President" of the Latter-day Saints and inaugurated a new era. He was the Colonel Harlan Sanders of Mormonism. He often wore white suits, had an infectious laugh, and understood the need to appeal to the world outside the Church. It was refreshing. Most LDS presidents had either been polygamist oddballs or stodgy old men in the eyes of the American public. McKay was more savvy, more media aware. He became so popular that film legend Cecil B. DeMille asked him to consult on the now classic movie *The Ten Commandments*.

Empowered by his personal popularity and by his sense that an opportune moment had come, McKay began refashioning the Church's image. He also began sharpening its focus. His famous challenge to his followers was, "Every Member a Missionary!" And the faithful got busy. It only helped that Ezra Taft Benson, a future Church president, was serving as the nation's secretary of agriculture under President Eisenhower. This brought respectability. It also helped that George Romney was the revered CEO of American Motors Corporation and that he would go on to be the governor of Michigan, a candidate for president of the United States, and finally a member of Richard Nixon's cabinet. This hinted at increasing power. The 1950s were good for Mormons.

Then came the 1960s. Like most religions, the LDS took a beating from the counterculture movement, but by the 1970s they were again on the rise. There was the Mormon Tabernacle Choir, a symbol of Americana when Americana was under siege. There was Mormon Donny Osmond's smile and Mormon Marie Osmond's everything and the three-year run of network television's *Donny and Marie* in the late 1970s that made words like *family, clean, talented, patriotic,* and even *cute* outshine some of the less-endearing labels laid upon the Saints through the years. New labels joined new symbols. A massive, otherworldly, 160,000-square-foot Temple just north of Washington, DC, was dedicated in the 1970s, a symbol of LDS power and permanence for the nation to behold. Always there was the "Every Member a Missionary!" vision beating in each Saintly heart.

By 1984, the dynamics of LDS growth were so fine-tuned that influential sociologist Rodney Stark made the mind-blowing prediction that the Latter-day Saints would have no fewer than 64 million members and perhaps as many as 267 million by 2080.[3] It must have seemed possible in those days. In the following ten years, LDS membership exploded from 4.4 million to 11 million. This may be why in 1998 the Southern Baptist Convention held its annual meeting in Salt Lake City. The Mormons—a misguided cult in the view of most traditional Christians, most Baptists in particular—had to be stopped.

They weren't. Four years after the Baptists besieged Temple Square, the Winter Olympic Games came to Salt Lake City. This was in 2002 and it is hard to exaggerate what this meant to the Latter-day Saints. A gifted Mormon leader, Mitt Romney, rescued the games after a disastrous bidding scandal. A sparkling Mormon city hosted the games. Happy, handsome, all-American Mormons attended each event, waving constantly to the cameras and appearing to be—in the word repeatedly used by the press at the time—"normal."

The LDS Church capitalized on it all. It sent volunteers, missionaries, and publicists scurrying to every venue. It hosted grand events for the world press. It made sure that every visitor received a brochure offering an LDS guided tour of the city. Visitors from around the world read these words: "No other place in America has a story to tell like that of Salt Lake City—a sanctuary founded by religious refugees from within the United States' own borders. And none can tell that story better than the Church of Jesus Christ of Latter-day Saints."[4] Largely unchallenged, the Mormon narrative prevailed.

What followed was the decade of the new millennium we have already surveyed. Mormons seemed to be everywhere, seemed to be exceptional in nearly every arena, seemed to have moved beyond *acceptance* by American culture to *domination* of American culture. At least this was what some feared at the time.

But Mormons did not dominate the country. Far from it. Remember that they were not even 2 percent of the nation's population as of 2012. True, they were visible and successful, well educated and well spoken, patriotic and ever willing to serve. Yet what they had achieved was not domination. It was not a conspiracy either, as some alleged. It was not anything approaching a takeover or even the hope for a takeover.

Few observers seemed to be able to explain how this new level of LDS prominence in American society came about. They reached for the usual answers trotted out to account for such occurrences: birth rates, Ronald Reagan's deification of traditional values, the economic boom of the late twentieth century, a more liberal and broadminded society, even the dumbing down of America through television and failing schools. Each of these explanations was found wanting.

———

The Mormon Machine

The truth lay within Mormonism itself. What the Saints had achieved in the United States was what Mormonism, unfettered and well led, will nearly always produce. This was the real story behind the much-touted "Mormon Moment." The Church of Jesus Christ of Latter-day Saints had risen to unexpected heights in American society because the Mormon religion creates what can benevolently be called a Mormon Machine— a system of individual empowerment, family investment, local church (ward and stake level) leadership, priesthood government, prophetic enduement, Temple sacraments, and sacrificial financial endowment of the holy Mormon cause.

Plant Mormonism in any country on earth and pretty much the same results will occur. If successful, it will produce deeply moral individuals who serve a religious vision centered upon achievement in this life. They will aggressively pursue the most advanced education possible, understand their lives in terms of overcoming obstacles, and eagerly serve the surrounding society. The family will be of supernatural importance to them, as will planning and investing for future generations. They will be devoted to community, store and save as a hedge against future hardship, and they will esteem work as a religious calling. They will submit to civil government and hope to take positions within it. They will have advantages in this. Their beliefs and their lives in all-encompassing community will condition them to thrive in administrative systems and hierarchies—a critical key to success in the modern world. Ever oriented to a corporate life and destiny, they will prize belonging and unity over individuality and conflict every time.

These hallmark values and behaviors—the habits that distinguish Mormons in the minds of millions of Americans—grow naturally from Mormon doctrine. They are also the values and behaviors of successful people. Observers who think of the religion as a cult—in the Jim Jones sense that a single, dynamic leader controls a larger body of devotees through fear, lies, and manipulation—usually fail to see this. Mormon doctrine is inviting, the community it produces enveloping and elevating, the lifestyle it encourages empowering in nearly every sense. Success, visibility, prosperity, and influence follow. *This is the engine of the Mormon ascent.* It is what has attracted so many millions, and it is the mechanism of the Latter-day Saints' impact upon American society and the world.

Engine #1—Progress: To Pass the Tests of Life

Ask a member of the Church of Jesus Christ of Latter-day Saints what he is devoted to in this life and he will likely answer that he is intent upon pleasing his Heavenly Father and becoming like Jesus Christ. Hearing this answer, atheists and agnostics roll their eyes and say, "Of course, that's the kind of thing all religious nutcases believe!" Traditional Christians, who use nearly the same language to answer the question, think this LDS Church member is keeping something from us, that there is more behind his statement of faith than he is willing to reveal. It usually is not so. He's telling us the truth, but for our purpose of understanding the Mormon impact upon America, it is the way that a Mormon seeks to please his Heavenly Father that tells the tale.

A Mormon believes he is in this world to pass tests. We'll talk more about why he thinks this a bit later, but for now it is important for us to know that Mormons believe that this life is like an obstacle course they must master in order to qualify for what comes in eternity. It is this word *qualify* that should be flashing bright red on the page. Mormon rituals and doctrines are filled with the language of accomplishment and achievement, possessed of the virtue of reaching goals and passing tests. Much of the terminology of Mormonism sounds like it comes from the handbook of the US Military Academy at West Point or from the textbooks of an elite MBA program.

In Mormonism, the Heavenly Father does not create matter; he organizes it. Mormons are meant to do likewise:

be like Heavenly Father in bringing order to the chaotic and lonely world, thus proving themselves worthy. The word *organize* is used again and again in Mormon sacred literature†, as are terms like *progress, pass the test, be found worthy, qualify, learn, make choices, prove, improve,* and—unceasingly—*make eternal progress*. Even the Church's magazine was once called *The Improvement Era* and for more than seventy years!

Laying aside the spiritual content of this vision for a moment, the fact that progress and achievement are at the heart of a Mormon's purpose on earth helps explain why Mormons are so adept at creating, leading, and even rescuing institutions. It is what they understand themselves to be on earth to do. It is the skill set required of their divine calling, and it is nearly the same skill set necessary for real-world success. In other words, there is a direct connection between Mormon beliefs and the triumph of the Marriott Corporation. There is a direct connection between Mormon theology and the remarkable success of Stephen Covey. There is an undeniable link between Mormon religious ideals and the fact that graduates of Brigham Young University are among the most sought after by the FBI, the CIA, the National Security Agency, the Secret Service, and hundreds of graduate schools around the country.

---

† Author Note: Telling the story of the Mormon journey in America inherently involves relying on a core of sources, the majority of which are official LDS materials. Since it would be tedious to cite these repeatedly in footnotes, an attempt has been made in this book to allude to the relevant source material in the natural flow of the narrative. These sources include the *Book of Mormon, Doctrine and Covenants, Pearl of Great Price, Joseph Smith's Biography,* Lucy Mack Smith's *Biography of Joseph Smith by His Mother* and Smith's *Church History*. In most cases, when quotations are made without formal citation, they refer to one of these well-known and oft-repeated sources. Occasionally, the author does cite a specific passage from one of these sources, but only when the author's case requires it. In addition to these citations and other endnotes, a bibliography for further reading is included at the end of the book.

Mormons make achievement through organizational management a religious virtue. It leads to prosperity, visibility, and power. It should come as no surprise, then, that an American can turn on the evening news after a day of work and find one report about two Mormon presidential candidates, another story about a Mormon finalist on *American Idol*, an examination of the controversial views of a leading Mormon news commentator, a sports story about what a Mormon lineman does with his "Temple garments" in the NFL, and a celebration of how Mormons respond to crises like Katrina and the BP oil spill, all by a "Where Are They Now?" segment about Gladys Knight, minus the Pips, who has become—of course—a Mormon.

Mormons rise in this life because it is what their religion calls for. Achieving. Progressing. Learning. Forward, upward motion. This is the lifeblood of earthly Mormonism. Management, leadership, and organizing are the essential skills of the faith. It is no wonder that Mormons have grown so rapidly and reached such stellar heights in American culture. And there is much more to come.

Engine #2—Family: For Time and All Eternity

Another fuel of the Mormon ascent in America—also a religious calling that wins secular success—is the priority of family and community. In LDS theology, the family is not only a sacred institution—something many religions claim—but it is an eternal institution. Mormons believe families existed together before they came to this world—in a state called "premortality"—and they will exist together as families throughout all eternity if they qualify. In fact, they will rule together one day as their Heavenly Father rules this world now with his family. This means that while American society as a whole is experiencing the destruction of the traditional family—with all the poverty, lost legacies, and broken lives that can result—Mormons are building large families that are passionately committed to a family destiny both in time and in eternity. In fact, the phrase *spiritual dynasty* is sometimes used.

The features of these thriving families are becoming better known as Mormons reach demographic critical mass. A Mormon mother and father believe that they were already joined before their life in this world began. They also already had children. They have a duty, they are taught, to make sure they give birth to enough bodies for all of their preexistent children. Mormon families, then, tend to be large. It is not uncommon for a professor at Brigham Young University to have eleven children. A family of thirteen children in a Mormon family is not unheard of. J. Willard Marriott, the founder of the hotel chain, was one of eight children. David Neeleman, the founder of JetBlue, is the father of nine. Stephen Covey, the management genius, is also the father of nine—and grandfather to fifty-two!

As important as the size of these families is the culture they create. If they remain true to Church teaching, children in these families will understand themselves as playing a vital role in an eternal family purpose. They will respect their parents, help their siblings, and embrace their family as almost the central priority of their lives—and not merely a tyranny to escape as soon as the law allows. None of these family members will drink alcohol, smoke, do drugs, have sex outside of marriage, or even drink caffeine. They will serve their Church and their community by way of serving their God. Parents will invest in the education of each child as a religious duty. All will attend meetings in which their eternal calling, unity, character, and purpose will be reinforced. Fatherhood, motherhood, sonship, and daughterhood will not be understood as the product of biology alone. They will be cherished as eternal spiritual states modeled after beloved heavenly beings. When the time is right, members of Mormon families will be "sealed" to each other "for time and all eternity" in sacred Temple ceremonies. The ties that bind will never be broken. Ever.

Engine #3—Education: Training the Saints to Lead

Connect families such as these at the local level and they will naturally begin devoting themselves to one of the great Mormon priorities—education, another engine of the Mormon ascent created out of a spiritual calling. In the same way that individual Mormons and their families are eternal, so too is what they learn in this life. One of the well-known LDS scriptures on this theme declares, "Whatever principle of intelligence we attain unto in this life, it will rise with us in the resurrection. And if a person gains more knowledge and intelligence in this life through his diligence and obedience than another, he will have so much the advantage in the world to come."[5] In other words, do your homework: you'll need what you learn in eternity.

Mormon education begins early and reaches tremendous heights. The Church Educational System (CES) offers a program called "primary" for younger children, operates a "seminary" for high school students to provide "eternal Mormon perspective" on what secular schools teach, and then maintains an "institute" that challenges college students to deeper faith. The LDS educational vision coalesces at Brigham Young University. Here, the Mormon devotion to education meets the calling to "prove worthy" and turns toward the challenge of the modern world. Most BYU students are upper tier academically, most are bilingual, most possess proven leadership gifts, and most intend to do graduate work. They not only complete an aggressive curriculum but also enroll in supplemental programs that fine-tune their skills. The attention to detail is impressive. Pre-law students can experience a professional etiquette dinner to learn what fork to use for the salad or how to make introductions at those White House dinners they plan to attend. MBA students can attend personal coaching sessions at the Marriott School of Management. Then, of course, there is the two-year missionary stint that most Mormon males undergo. It has been called the "boot camp of Mormon greatness." From all of these educational processes, the message is clear: "We intend to lead."

The Mormon culture of progress moves young Mormons to pursue education the way members of another religion might pursue heavenly visions. Graduate schools are full of Saints on their second or third advanced degree. Mitt Romney earned a law degree and an MBA and earned them both from Harvard—at the same time. US Senator Mike Lee's father was the founding dean of Brigham Young Law School. In addition to the seminary and institute required of all LDS high school and college students, Mike sat through family dinners that were regularly transformed into seminars on due process or the establishment clause. After these years, he earned an undergraduate degree from BYU, a law degree from BYU, became an Eagle Scout, clerked for a future US Supreme Court Justice, and somehow found two years in which to do his LDS missionary service in the Rio Grande Valley. No one was surprised when he ended up in the US Senate. He simply followed the Mormon way: *the impartation of family, the priority of education, the holy duty of service, the wisdom of networking, the eternal mandate to achieve.*

Engine #4—Patriotism: The Calling of the United States and the Free Market

Then there is the fiery patriotism inherent in Mormonism, which springs from the LDS certainty that the United States is divinely ordained. They draw this, first, from the Book of Mormon assertion that at least some of the ancient tribes in the New World were members of God's chosen people, the

Jews of Israel. That Jesus Christ appeared in America after his resurrection from the dead is confirmation of a special destiny. That the Book of Mormon was revealed in New York not long after the nation was born strengthens this view, as does the fact that the Garden of Eden, the spot upon which Jesus Christ will return to earth, and the headquarters of the true Church of Jesus Christ are all in the United States. Even the US Constitution is believed to be of divine origin. A treasured scripture finds Heavenly Father proclaiming, "And for this purpose have I established the Constitution of this land, by the hands of wise men who I raised up unto this very purpose."[6] Then, after Jesus Christ returns to earth, the world will be ruled from two Temples, one in Jerusalem and another in—Jackson County, Missouri.

Mormonism has spiritually riveted itself to the United States, so it is no surprise that Mormons have become super-patriots as a result. The Mormon Tabernacle Choir has sung at the inauguration of five presidents. Their Constitutional scholars, historians, and jurists have been among the most influential in the nation, particularly in recent decades. They, along with patriotic evangelicals, have tended the flame that illuminates a distinctly spiritual vision for the United States.

In recent years, this religious devotion to the United States has included a near-religious commitment to the free market system. It was not always so. Though in their early years Mormons were as devoted to free enterprise as they are today, they also esteemed economic equality, often embraced communal living, and strove for what one LDS historian described as "socialization of surplus incomes." They observed a stern Law of Consecration and Stewardship in which the faithful deeded— "consecrated"—all their property to the Church and were granted a smaller "stewardship" in return.[7] The first generation of Latter Day Saints was so convinced of its social obligations that it was used as an argument for the controversial practice of polygamy. The uncared-for woman would have a home. The impoverished widow would be welcomed into the largesse of a loving family. Even Joseph Smith, founder of the faith, married two elderly women merely to provide them care.

By contrast, the Latter-day Saints of today have been called "free-market apostles."[8] It was likely only a matter of time before this occurred, since free-market principles grow organically from Mormon soil. Their experience and their doctrines give them a fear of overreaching government, a devotion to volunteerism, an abhorrence of debt, a love of "hard" money, an admiration for thrift, a religious commitment to storing goods against the day of trouble, and, of course, a devotion to unfettered progress. There is also in LDS theology the guaranteed spiritual exchange that many Americans associate with the prosperity gospel of television preachers: that to serve God is to be rewarded, that righteous living draws divine blessing. It is little surprise, then, that Mormons run many of the nation's largest corporations. It is no surprise that Brigham Young University is becoming the Harvard of libertarian economics.

It is even less surprise that Mormons might supply most of the ground troops for free-market, multilevel enterprises like Amway and Mary Kay. And it is certainly no surprise that an LDS economist would insist that "Mormonism is the Protestant ethic on steroids."[9]

All of these—the ideal of progress, the power of family, the priority of education, and devotion to a divinely ordained America with its free-market heritage—have helped to fashion the engine of the Mormon advance in American society, the aid of their spiritual claims aside. They have each helped to create the celebrated "Mormon Moment."

———

The Spiritual Appeal of Mormonism

It is a mistake, though, to assume that Mormons have ascended for secular reasons alone. Their spiritual vision possesses a magnetic force of its own and many of the hundreds of thousands who become Saints after leaving other religions attest that this is so. This is likely a surprise for those who know Mormonism only by its extremes—its polygamy and its odd claims about history and its dreams of ruling as gods in universes yet unknown. We will journey through these mysteries in pages to come, but first we must understand that much of Mormonism's appeal to our age is found in the less extreme portions of its religious vision.

Heavenly Father

We live in an unfathered generation. The traditional family is dying. Divorce scars lives and scatters siblings. Absentee men leave their young in confused agony. The center does not hold. Loneliness, wounding, and isolation reign. To this Mormonism offers a Father. He is not a father-like God, loosely speaking, who is distant and uninvolved. He is a father in the most literal sense. He is married to Heavenly Mother and has given birth to all the spirits of humans on earth. In other words, the world is run by a loving family and every human being is part of it. In fact, each human belongs to a human family that was already assembled in love before coming to earth. Earthly life is about this family, which will continue through all eternity and eventually populate other planets just as Heavenly Father and Heavenly Mother have populated earth. This kind of belonging, this promise of happy relationships and the security of a supernaturally determined "place," is Mormonism's greatest appeal—and it reaches to modern society where it is perhaps most in need.

Spiritual Experience

We also live in a time of aching spiritual hunger. Religious institutions—what the young tend to call "organized religion"—have been found wanting. Our generation wearies of religion as thinly disguised politics, of religion as baptized vanity, of religion as sanctified greed, and of religion as meaningless ritual. To this, Mormonism offers spiritual experience and supernatural empowerment. Ask a seasoned Church member what is at the core of his faith and he is likely to say "the restoration of priesthood authority." This is what the faithful yearn for, what Mormons believe John the Baptist began in Joseph Smith, and what Peter, James, and John appeared shortly after to complete. This authority brings spiritual power and an "open heaven," a favorite LDS theme. Even their Temple architecture is designed to illustrate that the heavens are open to us.

The Mormon priesthood is a priesthood empowered, not only to teach and lead but to impart spiritual gifts and understand mysteries—even to heal. Outsiders who know only LDS order and buttoned-down ways find this a bit confusing. Yet Mormon history is dotted with meetings that make the first Day of Pentecost look tame. According to Church lore, Joseph Smith walked through encampments healing the sick. Brigham Young gave an entire sermon in unknown tongues while a second man interpreted for the crowd. It is common for a priesthood blessing to lead to a healing or a revelation. Mormons are so confident of spiritual experiences that its members are encouraged to become assured of Church teaching by "having a testimony"—LDS-speak for having a confirming experience or what some churches call "a witness of the Holy Spirit." Again, Mormonism reaches to a religiously suspicious society right at the point of a grinding need—with the promise of vital, immediate spiritual experience.

Unfolding Revelation

We live too in an age of doubt about absolute truth. We suspect any one-size-fits-all certainty. We prefer a postmodern what's-true-for-you-may-not-be-true-for-me customization. We want beliefs that evolve, that arc, that conform themselves to time, place, and feel. To this, Mormonism offers a religion of progressive revelation, a faith that rests on a Heavenly Father who is ever giving "new truth" even if it contradicts the "old truth" of revelations gone by. Consistency is not a problem.

The Church has a saying to explain this unfolding revelation: "A living prophet trumps a dead prophet." Joseph Smith may have a revelation that marriage to more than one wife is essential to reaching the highest heavens, but there is revelation to come. A later president—and all presidents are regarded by the faithful as prophets—claims a revelation that polygamy is sin. Soon, the Church prosecutes and even helps to imprison polygamist offenders. Initially in Mormon history, blacks are declared cursed, ugly, demonic, and barred from the Temple. This lasts for grinding generations. Yet, in 1978, it all goes away. And so it continues. Gays were once excommunicated, but now a gay man may assume his place in the Church as long as he remains celibate. More revelations are coming. There may even be scriptures to be found in a hill yet to be revealed. Women may one day enter the priesthood. New avenues may be found to the divine. It will only require a president or prophet to make it so, a new revelation, a progression of truth.

Here too the Saints reach to a need of American society—its deep-seated dream of ever-evolving truth.

The Problem of Mormon History

The Church of Jesus Christ of Latter-day Saints, then, has achieved startling influence in US society for two primary reasons: the secular success of the "Mormon Machine"— that is, the real-world benefits of the faith's religious require-ments—and the appeal of its spiritual claims for hurting souls in a troubled age. But there are challenges ahead. All may not continue to be as it has been.

With growing size and visibility will come fresh scrutiny of the soft underbelly of the Church: its history. Mormonism is a historical faith. It makes spiritual assertions rooted in specific claims about earthly events. This moves its theology out of the realm of faith alone and subjects it to intrusive matters like historical research, scientific evidence, and medical testing. It is not a challenge the Church leadership, not to mention the average Mormon—despite his intense training—is prepared for. It will likely present a crisis to the faithful unlike any they have known. It will come into their lives and the lives of their children through the Internet and the personalized media of our age. It will probe the cracks left by an LDS educational system that is "faith promoting," not designed for the demands of intellectual combat. It will require innovative thinking by

Mormon leadership and it may even force an openness that could change the Church forever.

A brief story illustrates this. A researcher visiting the University of Utah interviews an LDS professor about the history of his faith. They have a pleasant exchange and then the professor has something to ask: "Why do some Christians call us a cult? Don't they know this is hurtful?" The researcher is taken aback. Hurtful? It seems almost benign by comparison. To answer the professor's question, the non-Mormon gently reminds the Saint of his own history.

In the First Vision of Joseph Smith as it is taught by the LDS Church, God the Father and Jesus Christ appeared and said that all previous versions of Christianity were "corrupt" and an "abomination" in God's eyes. This meant the early Christians who rescued abandoned babies from atop Roman walls and Telemachus, who died bringing an end to the bloody coliseum games. It meant the Celtic monks who protected the intellectual heritage of the West during the Dark Ages and monks who took care of the insane and medieval orders that created hospitals. It meant Saint Francis of Assisi and Martin Luther and the hymn writer Isaac Watts. It meant those who were burned at the stake for translating the Bible and Moravians who sold themselves into bondage to tend the needs of African slaves. All corrupt and abominable? Then, when the Church formed, it branded itself "the only true and living Church." Jesus was pleased with no other. There was no uncertainty here. In fact, non-Mormon clergy were depicted in

Temple rituals as serving the devil until not long ago. Even today they are called "sectarian ministers" by the LDS faithful. And let's not forget that all non-Mormons are called "gentiles," a term taken from the history of Jews that means "those outside the covenants of God."

Still, to their credit, the Saints do believe that members of other churches can be saved—*if they become Mormons in the next life!*

It is an uncomfortable moment. The professor is troubled and says he understands there is offense on both sides. What he does not see, though, is that while he perceives Mormon history to have been explained or outlived or somehow risen above, that history still speaks to the outside world. The questions of that world—indeed, its demands for explanation—are not going away.

———

Joseph Smith

Nowhere is this more an obstacle to Mormon aspirations than when it comes to Joseph Smith, the LDS founder. For the faithful he is the true prophet of the true word of God to the true Church. He is noble and holy and good. He is Heavenly Father's chosen vessel.

To much of the outside world, Joseph Smith is viewed as both a deceiver and himself deceived. He made part of his living through occult practices, something the LDS Church itself would condemn among the faithful today. His wife's father despised him and was embarrassed that his son-in-law was treasure hunting and seeking revelations in rocks—"seer stones," they were called. Smith later used these same seer stones to translate the Book of Mormon. He put the stones in the bottom of his hat and then followed them with his face, dictating what he saw to a scribe. He had been criminally tried for something like this practice just a few years before.

Once he founded the Church, Smith guided it by exceptionally convenient revelations. He claimed revelations that told the faithful they should build him a house, that told a fourteen-year-old girl she should marry him, that told all the Saints polygamy was necessary to obtain the highest level of salvation, that told his wife to obey him or Heavenly Father would destroy her, and that told the Church he and his family should always have rooms in the LDS hotel. He bought some old mummies and something that looked like Egyptian papyri from a peddler passing through Ohio. Soon after he announced that he had translated the papyri and that they contained the writings of the patriarch Abraham. Non-LDS Egyptologists laugh at the tale—and the translation. Yet it is the basis for Smith's *Book of Abraham*, which is regarded as Scripture by the Church today. Several of his closest friends—some of whom said they were with him during visitations by John the Baptist or the apostles Peter, James, and John—accused him of adultery. His wife threw several women out of her house and cursed them for overfamiliarity with her husband. She didn't know the women were her husband's other wives. Few of his friends were still with him in the end.

Hardly any of these facts are disputed by LDS historians and a similar rant could be drawn from the life of Brigham Young. Or from the saga of polygamy. Or from the murders at Mountain Meadows. Or from the lack of evidence for Book of Mormon claims. Or even from the Mormon insistence upon symbolically baptizing dead Jews, a practice so recent that Holocaust survivor and Nobel Laureate Elie Wiesel felt compelled to call for the end of it on the day these words were written.

Of course, the lives of Smith and Young—indeed all of LDS history—could be recounted as a more inspiring, far nobler tale. Much of it was. Still, Americans are a people addicted to evidence, and Mormons will never be able to avoid confrontation with their past or with other Americans over their past. There is too much contradiction, too much that is human passed off as divine, too much still waiting to be answered. And the average Mormon is unprepared to give an answer. His education has been limited to what is "faith promoting." He simply has not been equipped for the controversies surrounding his Church.

Questions for the Present Mormon Moment

This brilliant moment of Mormonism at the center of the national stage, then, is a time when the Saints may lift their heads and tearfully honor what their ancestors won for them, what their faith produces for them, and how they have grasped the opportunities at hand in their own time. It is, and should be, a moment of celebration.

Yet it is also, and must be, a moment of confrontation with the kind of hard-hitting questions that being so many millions and wielding such influence brings. Does the teaching of the Church stand up to modern science? To what we know about history? Was Joseph Smith a charlatan and a liar? Will a Church spiritually and physically welded to the United States maintain control of the majority of its members who live in other countries? How will twenty-first-century Mormons answer for the extremes of their nineteenth-century ancestors? Is it possible Mormons have reached great heights in American culture because Mormonism is a religion *of* American culture, because Joseph Smith ingeniously wove a religion from the finest features of the nation in the first decades of its life? How is its new visibility going to change the LDS Church? What traditional doctrines will be abandoned? What new doctrines will be added?

These are questions the recent Mormon rise to influence presses on the faithful. It is vital that a new LDS generation respond, for this too is part of the present Mormon Moment— that a modern Church of Jesus Christ of Latter-day Saints make a reasoned case for its presence on the American stage.

CHAPTER 1

THE MORMON VIEW OF MORMONISM

I have trouble getting my head around the Mormons. . . . The history strikes me somewhere between incredulity and horror, from golden plates in upstate New York to massacres out West. The theology comes across as totally barmy. We can become gods with our own planets! And the practices strike me as creepy. No coffee and tea is bad enough. But the underwear![1]

—Michael Ruse, philosopher

Hugh Riddick has been preparing for this conversation with his grandson almost his entire life. It is a conversation fathers and sons, grandfathers and grandsons have been having in his family for most of the 180-year history of the Latter-day Saints. Now, Hugh will have a chance to help prepare a new generation of Riddicks for the true priesthood of God—just as soon as young Jacob cleans up from his baseball game.

Jacob Riddick is thirteen and tomorrow he will take his first steps toward priesthood. His father was a priest, Hugh—his grandfather—is a priest, and so it has been since Brigham

Young led the Saints. This is what it means to be a male member of the Church of Jesus Christ of Latter-day Saints. This is what it means to be a Mormon man.

Hugh would have been happy to hear about this conversation secondhand. He would rather that his own son, David, had been here to guide Jacob. But David had chosen to be a US Marine. It was what he wanted to be from the time he was a little boy and Hugh was never able to change his mind. Perhaps he should not have tried. David was a "warrior's warrior," they said, and he rose rapidly in the ranks. That's what landed him in Iraq at the forefront of Operation Phantom Fury during the Second Battle of Fallujah. Command knew that he would lead well. And he did, but David was killed on the third day, November 11, 2004—Veteran's Day. Each year since, that flag-waving, parade-filled holiday has tortured Hugh Riddick and his wife.

Now, though, Hugh is sitting on his back porch enjoying the cool breeze off the pond and waiting for Jacob. When the boy appears, he does not look anything like anyone's image of a priest. He's wearing gym shorts and a T-shirt, his hair is wet and slicked back, and he has a slight bluish mustache from the powdered drink he's been guzzling. He sits down in a rocker, crosses his legs Indian-style in the seat, and takes another sip of his drink. Hugh just smiles. He knows that in spiritual things, appearances do not matter.

"How'd it go, sport?"

"We won. Wasn't that hard. They pretty much caved."

"I see. How'd you hit?"

"Two doubles and thrown out at first."

"Good! Nice going. Any RBIs?"

"Just one. And just barely, 'cause Danny Tomkins is so stinking slow!"

"Oh, I remember him. Runs like he's carrying a ton of bricks. Well, good job batting him in, buddy. Okay, you ready to talk?"

"Yes, sir."

"Do you know what's going to happen tomorrow, Jacob?"

"Of course, Pawpaw. I'm going to become a deacon."

"Yes. That's right. And do you understand what that means?"

"It's the first step to becoming a priest. It means that one day I'm going to be part of the priesthood that Heavenly Father restored in the time of Joseph Smith. It means I'm being prepared to receive priesthood authority."

"You've been listening closely to Elder Clarke, haven't you? That's right: tomorrow you will become a deacon. Do you know what that word really means?"

"Uh, I think I do. It means, like, servant or someone who takes care of something, right?"

"That's it. Perfect. It means someone who serves. And after you're ordained, you will be allowed to serve by passing out the bread and the water in the sacrament meetings and serving the priesthood leaders in various ways and helping keep the meeting house in order and so on, right?"

"Yes, sir."

"And then what?"

"Well, if I prove myself, in a couple of years I may be able to become a teacher. Then I can fill the sacramental trays and go with someone on home teaching visits and stuff like that. Then, maybe a couple of years after that, if I qualify, I can be a priest."

"Good. That's pretty much right. And all this is part of what? Do you know?"

"The Aaronic Priesthood, right?"

"Yes. Good, but Jacob, I don't want these just to be words to you. I want you to understand how much all this means. Not long after Jesus Christ lived on earth, the church lost its authority. It was corrupt and had warped doctrine. And so for centuries the Christian church was in darkness and chaos. It was a horrible time and Heavenly Father was deeply displeased. Then, finally, priesthood authority was restored. And you know about all that, right? You know that story?"

"Yes, sir. About the visitations from John the Baptist and Peter and James and John?"

"Yes, very good. So it is important for you to understand that this is all very important. Latter Day Saints died for this gift, Jacob. Your ancestors were slaughtered at places like Haun's Mill and Carthage for having this gift. You were determined for this before you came to this world. This is how Heavenly Father's plan for you is to unfold and how you become what you are made to be for all eternity. I'm hoping you progress on to the Melchizedek Priesthood and then, perhaps, to high priest and even further from there."

Jacob looks out at the pond. Hugh thinks perhaps he has given the boy more than he can absorb, but then he notices that Jacob's eyes are moist.

"Pawpaw," the boy says in a fractured voice, "what kind of priest was my dad?"

Hugh has to look away from Jacob to answer. The searching in the boy's eyes is too much. "He was going to be given the Melchizedek Priesthood when he came home, Jacob. He died before he could receive it."

Jacob ponders this for a few moments and then says, "I want to be whatever he couldn't be because he died, Pawpaw. I want to make it to the level he would have reached and then do it for him."

Hugh is too moved by this to speak. Jacob, seeing his grandfather's emotion, sets down his drink, gets up from his chair, and puts his arms around the man he loves most in the world.

"You make me proud, Jacob," Hugh says through tears, holding his grandson tightly. "Yes, do it for your daddy and all the Riddicks. And do it for the Latter-day Saints."

It is one of the great ironies of the Church of Jesus Christ of Latter-day Saints that while outsiders perceive it largely in terms of its unusual doctrines, the Saints see themselves in a completely different light. The outer world focuses, for example, on matters like polygamy. "Holy underwear" is also a favorite topic, as is their aspiration to divinity and their belief that God was once a man. The century and a half they banned blacks from their Temple and priesthood is much discussed. So is the iron-fisted rule from LDS headquarters at Salt Lake City's Temple Square. The Mormon opposition to California's Proposition 8 has made them look homophobic, their insistence upon being baptized for Jewish Holocaust survivors has made them look cruel, and their standard missionary presentation has made them look mindlessly robotic. All of these novelties frame the perceptions of Mormons in the wider world.

Ask a Saint about any of these, though, and an expression of confusion will likely flash fleetingly across his face. He knows that each is part of the Mormon matrix but he likely does not think of any as vital. Doctrine is not primary for him; experience is. The prophecies and the ordinances and the revelations from Heavenly Father are what make up his religion. Most of the doctrines so often discussed in the press are at the edge of his experience and are rarely on his mind.

Let him speak for a moment about his own Mormon experience and a far different picture will likely emerge. He may very well talk about what home teaching is like and how dear the community of the Saints has become. He'll likely describe, even with tears, how he's raising his children to be holy. If he is trusting, he will tell of the time he was sick and a priesthood blessing made him well. He may even speak, loosely, of his sealing to his wife for time and all eternity and of the endowment ceremony he has gone through. He will not give details, of course, but he will still make his point. It is not the doctrines that have won him. He sometimes isn't even sure what all of them are. It's the supernatural empowering of a holy community that is most important to him.

This is the great disconnect between how Mormons understand themselves and then how the rest of the world perceives them. It is easy to see the Latter-day Saints as extremists drawn to extreme teachings, as the descendants of a nineteenth-century cult who are now trying to give their scraggly batch of doctrines a modern, high-tech, public relations overhaul. Whatever truth there may be in this, it misses the central point of Mormonism as Mormons themselves try to live it. And this, in the end, is the version of Mormonism that is going to prevail in the coming century—the version the Saints are living out while asking others to join them.

What Matters to a Mormon

For a Latter-day Saint, the heart of Mormonism is the restoration of priesthood authority. It is impossible to overstate this. At the core of everything Saintly is the unshakable belief that something lost for centuries was restored through Joseph Smith. It is now present in the modern world. It is present only through the LDS Church. It is what all men will ultimately need.

Mormons believe that the pure Christianity of Jesus Christ lasted only a short while after Jesus left this life. The Christian church quickly became unrighteous and corrupt, and it stayed that way until around 1830. In other words, for centuries the Christian church was a perverse shell of what was intended. Then came Joseph Smith. He not only gave the world the Book of Mormon, but he also received, along with a man named Oliver Cowdery, the restoration of the true priesthood of God. Mormons speak of this as a restoration of "priesthood authority," which they believe was given in two defining appearances by glorified human beings: an appearance by John the Baptist and an appearance by the apostles Peter, John, and James. In these appearances or "visitations," the only real priesthood was restored—to Mormons.

This means that when someone asks, "Where has the great age of miracles and revelation gone?" The Church of Jesus Christ of Latter-day Saints says, "It is here, right now, with us." What Mormons believe they have in this "priesthood authority" is the ability to "bring Jesus Christ into people's lives" through "ordinances." It is the ability to give the gifts of the Holy Spirit, to have revelations, to bless, to dedicate, and even to heal. In other words, it is the supernatural power to do the "great works" that were done before the Christian church went astray.

The Heart of the Faith

Of course, the nonreligious think this is crazy. The traditional Christian thinks it is devilish. The Jew thinks it is evidence of a stolen legacy. And nearly non-Mormon thinks it is fruit of an astonishing Mormon arrogance.

Still, it is one of the most important truths we can know about what Mormonism is. Despite Joseph Smith's many doctrinal innovations, Mormonism is not primarily about doctrine. It is about the experience of a restored supernatural power, the all-important matter of "priesthood authority." This was what Smith built upon. It is what early Mormons sought. It is still at the heart of the faith. It is what outsiders most misunderstand.

Though it is risky to make the comparison, the best illustration of this vital truth is found in the thinking of the Prophet Muhammad, whom Joseph Smith deeply admired. For a man living in the sixth century, Muhammad was well traveled. His occupation for many years was leading caravans that crossed the known world carrying goods from place to place. This brought the future prophet into contact with nearly all the religions of his day. He likely sat by the campfires of Jews and Christians of every type and heard them talk about what they believed. He admired them both, but their factions and theological divisions disturbed him. Jews rallied around their rabbis and Christians rallied around their favorite theologies and even slew each other over seemingly slight doctrinal matters.

Muhammad found it all too complex, too contentious. When he began claiming to have revelations and when this set him to the task of designing a new religion, he decided that simplicity was the key. It should be simple to get into the faith and simple to understand the main doctrines of the faith. The more difficult matter would be actually living it out.

The simplicity of Islam has historically been part of its power. A man enters Islam largely through a one-sentence confession, the Shahadah—"There is no God but Allah and Muhammad is his prophet"—and then understands the core of Islam with "Five Pillars" that describe his duties and "Six Articles of Faith" that describe his beliefs. This is the heart of Islam. And the genius. Islam conquered a huge portion of the known world in the first hundred years of its existence partially through the power of the sword and partially through the simplicity of its system. In this matter of simplicity, Islam was to religion what McDonald's is to food: easily remembered, easily consumed, easily replicated.

Though Mormons won't necessarily feel complimented by the comparison, Joseph Smith was much like Muhammad in this popularizing, simplifying work. Dr. Kathryn Flake, a Mormon who is also an esteemed professor at Vanderbilt University, has said, "Joseph Smith was the Henry Ford of revelation. He wanted every home to have one, and the revelation he had in mind was the revelation he'd had, which was seeing God."[2] Dr. Flake is referring to the same dynamic in the intent of Joseph Smith that we've seen in the doctrinal system of Muhammad. Though Mormonism appears complex to the outsider, it was actually an attempt to be something like the McDonald's of American religion.

Smith lived at a time of great spiritual upheaval, excitement, and division—as we'll see in the next chapter. Like Muhammad, he was put off by the constant bickering in Christianity. He claimed revelations in which he was told that all churches were corrupt, that none of them had the truth, and that none were worth joining. He wanted his "true Church" to move beyond everything that led to the infighting and destruction he had seen among Christians. This created the Mormonism we know today.

The faith of the Saints evolved by prophecy rather than by doctrine. Smith was opposed to creeds. He thought they were little more than invitations to a fight. As a result, today it is difficult to find a definitive, systematic statement of what Mormons believe produced by the Mormons themselves. By their critics? Yes. By Mormons? No. He also thought that a paid clergy is an abomination—he called them "hireling priests" who would "feed themselves, not the flock"—so most Mormon leaders are unpaid volunteers. They are also untrained theologically. The study of doctrine is surprisingly informal in the Church. As a result, there is little place for professional theologians among the Saints, unlike some denominations in which the theologians almost outnumber the members. And though there are dozens of titles a male Mormon can wear—from deacon to bishop, from high priest to president—none of them come with any academic requirements.

All of this stems from the fact that Joseph Smith was focused more on what a man does than on what he believes. He was interested in spiritual experience, not theories about the spiritual. He wanted revelations, not theologies; an open heaven, not just open books. "Deeds, not creeds," the Saints often say, and this is the intentional legacy of Joseph Smith.

The result is that while the outside world naturally identifies Mormons by the doctrinal oddities they have accrued through the years, Mormons think of themselves in terms of priesthood authority and the sacred life they share together as a result of this grand restoration.

The Mormons and the Media

Nowhere in American society does this create an occasion of people talking past each other as when it comes to the media pursuing a prominent Mormon.

Reporters naturally want to find something controversial about this visible person, so they ask about holy underwear. But the Mormon won't answer this question directly. He's offended by the phrase "holy underwear"—it is properly called a "Temple garment"—and he won't talk about Temple rituals in any case because they are far too sacred. Besides, betraying Temple rituals is forbidden.

Then the media switches to polygamy. This too gets side-stepped because the Church forbade polygamy long before this prominent Mormon was born and only a small percentage of Saints have ever been in plural marriages to begin with. There's nothing to write about here.

Reporters then raise the treatment of blacks. This may get some play because the Latter-day Saints did not "get a revelation" about blacks being priests and permitted in the Temple until 1978. Even the Supreme Court moved toward equality faster than the Church of Jesus Christ of Latter-day Saints! So the media can stir these waters a bit, but the change came forty-five years ago and everybody has admitted the Church was wrong and even African American Mormons will criticize the media if it does not report fairly where the Church is today.

Then there is abortion and homosexuality, but more than half the country is with the Mormons on this so there is nothing new to spin. There is some fun to be had with the Mormon anti-birth-control position, but this is old and not all Mormons accept it and it will only bring Mormon women to the cameras in a rage. Better to leave this alone too.

It also doesn't work to bring up specific matters of doctrine. Press a political candidate on whether Jesus will touch down in Jackson County, Missouri, when he returns and the man either answers incorrectly or says he doesn't know. Ask if he intends to be a god one day and he says his faith doesn't make this clear. Ask if he thinks he will rule over planets and he laughs and says that some members of his faith believe this.

The man cannot be pinned down, though, and this is because Mormon doctrine is dangerous territory. It is always a bit—*squishy*. There is no creed. There are few if any LDS theologians. The clergy isn't theologically trained. The people are usually only taught what is "faith promoting" so there are huge gaps in what they know. And in Mormonism there is nothing like the Roman Catholic "Congregation for the Doctrine of the Faith"—no official voice, no department clarifying theology and whipping dissidents back into line. So the candidate moves deftly around the icebergs that reporters try to put in his way.

Then there are always conspiracy theories to pose about how much Salt Lake City controls a leading politician or how much money the church spends trying to turn elections their way. But no one knows for sure and there is such a mind meld between the Church and its prominent members that there is hardly need for the Church to even try to exert control. These Mormons all think so alike that nothing ever has to be said.

And this is where it usually stops. Because the media only knows Mormonism by its odd extremities, it exhausts its list of interesting topics quickly. The reporting becomes vapid. Religion moves from center stage. The fact that a CEO or a politician or a cabinet member or some other influential member of society might be a Mormon is no longer deemed important.

Because the media is focused on externals. Because the sordid burns out quickly. Because no one has thought to ask a Mormon what it really means to be a Mormon.

Yet when the Saints are approached in the light by which they see themselves—as the only earthly heirs of the ancient priesthood of Aaron and Melchizedek—then a new list of questions begins to emerge.

"Sir, your Church is offended when it is called a 'cult.' But if your Church sees itself as the 'only true Church,' possessors of the only true priesthood on earth, then don't Mormons see every other religion in the world as some kind of cult?"

"Sir, if you are a Melchizedek Priest, have you ever prayed for anyone to be healed? Have they been? Have you ever seen angels? Can you confer the gifts of the Holy Spirit? Can you confer them on me?"

"Sir, are there prophets who speak to you regularly? Do you prophesy to others? What will you do if someone you revere as a prophet gives you a revelation about what you should do in a public office? How can you refuse it? How can you be sure it is or isn't the true word of God?"

"Sir, if your Church has been given the keys to the only true Aaronic and Melchizedek Priesthoods on earth, then what does this say about the Jews? Are they deceived about who they are? And does becoming a Mormon literally change a person's blood so they become the seed of Abraham, as Joseph Smith taught? And who exactly will be in control of Jerusalem when Jesus Christ returns?"

These, then, are questions nearer the meaning of Mormonism that the Saints themselves hold dear and these get us closer to understanding how an LDS politician or CEO or educator understands both his public life as well as his life in this world.

What the Mormon view of Mormonism also tells us is how we have to approach the faith. There is no Mormon systematic theology or final theological voice. The text of Mormonism is Mormon history. In fact, there is a direct connection between each major phase of the Mormon past and what most every Mormon believes and practices today. But the story has to be told and its meaning understood.

This has not been easy for most Americans. Not only is religion of any kind seldom taught in our schools, but Mormon history is such an odd creature that it requires a certain openness, a willingness to take seriously—even for a moment— a story our Mormon friends believe was begun by angels, powered by prophecy, sustained by miracles, and made heroic by men destined to be divine. This history, though, is the main text of the faith that has now reached critical mass in the United States and it is well worth considering for this reason alone.

A Mormon Chronology

Circa 600 BC	An Israelite named Lehi travels with his family from the Middle East to the Americas. His descendants become the ever-warring Nephites and Lamanites.
AD 33	Jesus Christ appears to the Nephites immediately after his resurrection. This leads to several centuries of peace between the Nephites and the Lamanites before conflict resumes.
AD 385	Mormon, a prophet among the Nephites, gives a nearly completed work of his people to his son, Moroni, who finishes the work in AD 421, imprints them on plates of gold, and buries them in a hill named Cumorah.
1801	**June 1**: Brigham Young is born to a farm family in Whitingham, Vermont. He is the ninth of eleven children.
1805	**December 23**: Joseph Smith is born in Sharon, Vermont, the fifth child of Lucy and Joseph Smith.

1811	After difficult years, the Smith family moves to Lebanon, New Hampshire, where their financial condition improves and the Smith children are able to attend school.
1812	During a widespread typhoid epidemic that kills more than 6,000 people, Joseph Jr. develops a painful leg infection, which he survives only after a traumatic surgery and months of recovery. He walks with a limp the rest of his life.
1816	After three years of devastating crop failure, the Smith family moves to Palmyra, New York. The town of 4,000 is in the "burned-over district" where waves of religious revivals have left both spiritual excitement and theological confusion in their wake.
1820	**Spring**: While Smith is praying in a grove one morning, God the Father and his son, Jesus Christ, appear. They forgive Smith's sins and tell him that all Christian churches are abominations and corrupt and that he should not join any of them. Mormons call this "The First Vision."
1823	**September 21**: The angel Moroni appears to Smith and tells him of a book imprinted on gold plates buried in a nearby hillside. The next day, Smith discovers the plates three miles from the family farm but is told he is not ready to receive them yet, that he must return each September 22 for four years.

1827	**January 18**: Joseph Smith marries Emma Hale.
	September 22: His four-year wait concluded, Smith receives the gold plates from Moroni along with distinctive spectacles that allow him to translate the "Reformed Egyptian" language in which the narrative on the plates is written.
	December: The Smiths move to Harmony, Pennsylvania.
1828	Joseph begins translating the plates with the aid of Martin Harris.
	July: Smith first records a revelation.
1829	**May 15**: During the months required to translate the golden plates, Smith and Oliver Crowdery, a schoolteacher who assists Smith, receive a visitation from John the Baptist. He confers on Smith and Crowdery the Aaronic Priesthood and tells them that the Melchizedek Priesthood will also be conferred soon, leading to the creation of the true church over which Smith will be First Elder. After the visitation, Smith and Crowdery baptize each other in the Susquehanna River.
	June: The translation of the Book of Mormon is completed.
	Several days after John the Baptist's appearance, the apostles Peter, James, and John appeared to Smith and Crowdery, ordained them to the Melchizedek Priesthood, and bestowed on them the gifts of the Holy Spirit.

1830	**March 26**: The Book of Mormon is published. **April 6**: In Fayette, New York, Smith, Crowdery, and four others organize a new church and name Smith "Elder of the Church of Jesus Christ of Latter-day Saints." **June**: Moses appears to Smith in a vision. **October**: Smith receives a vision instructing him to move the church to Kirtland, Ohio, where missionaries have already won numerous converts.
1831	**June**: Keeping his headquarters in Kirtland, Smith moves bands of Mormons west to Independence, Missouri, the "New Jerusalem" where the faithful are to build a Temple. The cornerstone of that Temple is laid in August. **July 20**: Jackson County, Missouri, is designated as "Zion."
1832	**March 24**: Smith is tarred and feathered in Kirtland. Brigham Young joins the Saints as a convert in Kirtland. **April to June**: Smith visits Jackson County, Missouri.
1833	The *Book of Commandments*, a volume of Smith's revelations, is published.

1833	**July 23**: The cornerstones for the first Mormon Temple are laid in Kirtland.
	July: Mormons told they must leave Jackson County.
	November: Missouri Mormons are expelled from Jackson County.
1834	**April 24–30**: Rumors of a great Mormon army move a Missouri mob to burn 150 Mormon houses.
1835	**July**: Smith purchases Egyptian mummies and papyri, the latter of which, once translated, becomes *The Book of Abraham*.
	August: The Church issues the first of a number of denials that it is practicing polygamy.
	February 14: "The Quorum of the Twelve Apostles" is organized.
	The Doctrine and Covenants is published. It incorporates the sixty-five revelations of *The Book of Commandments* into its 138 revelations and includes seven Smith lectures.
1836	**March 27**: A week of dedication of the Kirtland Temple begins.
1837	The first mission to Great Britain begins.

1838	**June**: To resist persecution in Missouri, the Mormons organize the "Sons of Dan," or the "Danites," who gain a reputation in the press as "Destroying Angels." **August 6**: After a skirmish over voting rights, Governor Boggs of Missouri orders that the Mormons must be "exterminated or driven from the state." It is the only extermination order against a religion ever issued in the United States. **October 30**: Incited by the Missouri governor's extermination decree, a mob kills seventeen Mormons at Haun's Mill. Children number among the dead. Joseph Smith is arrested and sentenced to death. He is saved only by the commanding officer's refusal to carry out his sentence. Smith spends five months in prison.
1839	**April**: Smith is allowed to escape. Soon after, he establishes the city of Nauvoo on the banks of the Mississippi River in Illinois. Within five years Nauvoo rivals Chicago in population. The Mormon militia, 5,000 strong, inspires fear among non-Mormons in the region. **November 29**: Smith meets with President Martin Van Buren and demands compensation for Mormon property losses in Missouri.
1840	**December 16**: The Illinois legislature grants Nauvoo a charter allowing for exceptional local control and political liberty.

1841	Smith marries Louisa Beaman, the first of many "plural wives."
1842	**March 15**: Due to Freemasonry's influence upon Joseph Smith, a Masonic Lodge is built in Nauvoo. Smith devises the Temple ordinances, later known as "endowments," that are central to Mormon practice and reflect the distinct Masonic worldview and practice. **March 17**: The Relief Society, a women's social aid organization, is organized.
1843	**May 28**: Smith is "sealed" to his wife Emma Hale Smith for eternity. **July 12**: The Prophet teaches two new doctrines—baptism for the dead and polygamy—which prompts some to leave the Church.
1844	**January 29**: Smith declares himself a candidate for president of the United States. **March 11**: The Council of Fifty is organized. **April 7**: Smith gives his famous "King Follet Discourse," in which he proclaims that God has a physical body, that God was once a man, that men may become gods, that matter is eternal, and that the dead may be saved by the "sealing power" of the Latter Day Saints.

1844	**April 11**: The Council of Fifty anoints Smith "King, Priest and Ruler over Israel on Earth." **June 25**: Smith surrenders himself to authorities after ordering the destruction of an opposition newspaper, the *Nauvoo Expositor*. **June 27**: Joseph Smith and his brother, Hyrum, are killed in their jail cell by an anti-Mormon mob. The Latter Day Saints number 26,000 members. **August 8**: Brigham Young, the president of the Quorum of the Twelve Apostles, assumes leadership of the Church.
1845	**January**: The Illinois Legislature revokes Nauvoo's charter. **September 4**: Young and the Twelve agree to leave Illinois "as soon as grass grows and water runs."
1846	**February 4**: Thousands of Mormons begin moving west to escape persecution. **April 30**: The Temple at Nauvoo is dedicated. In the months that follow, vast numbers of Latter Day Saints receive their "endowments" and many polygamous marriages are "sealed." **August**: Winter Quarters are established near the present site of Florence, Nebraska.

1847	**July 24**: The Latter Day Saints first enter the Great Salt Lake Valley. The day is celebrated as Pioneer Day by later generations.
1848	Thousands of Mormons arrive in the Great Salt Lake Valley to create a "kingdom in the tops of the mountains."
1849	The territory of Utah is established by the US Congress.
1850	Brigham Young is made the governor of the Utah territory.
1852	Polygamy is first proclaimed outside of the Mormon Church, which leads to fierce condemnation of the Latter Day Saints and urgent calls for government intervention.
1853	**April 6**: The Reorganized Church of Jesus Christ of Latter Day Saints is formed by Mormons who reject polygamy and believe the Church should only be led by members of the Smith family. Headquartered in Independence, Missouri, it is supported by Joseph Smith's first wife, Emma, and eventually led by Smith's eldest son. **February 14**: A groundbreaking ceremony takes place for the Temple at Salt Lake City. Construction will take forty years.

1857	**September**: The Mountain Meadows massacre, in which 120 members of an Arkansas wagon train are killed, stains the reputation of Mormons nationwide and raises lasting questions about Brigham Young's complicity.
1858	Federal troops march into Salt Lake City, ending what President Buchanan calls "The Mormon War." It is a war largely over polygamy, which continues in the territory for decades more.
1862	The Morrill Anti-Bigamy Act criminalizes polygamy in US Territories. Abraham Lincoln refuses to enforce it.
1866	The Latter-day Saints grow to 60,000 members.
1877	**March 23**: John D. Lee, the instigator of the Mountain Meadows massacre, is executed. **August 29**: Brigham Young dies. More than 50,000 people attend his funeral. The Latter-day Saints now number over 100,000 members.
1887	The Edmunds-Tucker Act disincorporates the Mormon Church and allows the US government to confiscate all church property valued above $50,000. The US Supreme Court upholds the Act.

1890	**September 25**: LDS president Wilford Woodruff renounces polygamy.
1894	The Mormon Church numbers well over 200,000 members.
1896	**January 4**: Utah becomes the forty-sixth state in the American Union.
1904	The LDS church excommunicates polygamists and aids the US government in prosecuting offenders. Reed Smoot, an LDS Apostle, is elected to the US Senate. Anti-Mormon sentiment inflames confirmation hearings that stretch over three years. Smoot's ultimate confirmation is an early sign of growing acceptance for Latter-day Saints in American society.

CHAPTER 2

IN SEARCH OF TRUE RELIGION

Mormonism, as it is called, must stand or fall on the story of Joseph Smith. He was either a prophet of God, divinely called, properly appointed and commissioned, or he was one of the biggest frauds this world has ever seen. There is no middle ground.[1]

—Joseph F. Smith, LDS President

It is a bright first Sunday in April and Jenny Mills cannot wait for this morning's meeting to start. It is Testimony Sunday. She has been fasting. The Spirit has given her an impression. Now, finally, on Testimony Sunday, she will declare her faith.

She has watched these special days come and go through the years but never has she felt that special prompting. She knows what it is, though. She visited Temple Square years ago with her parents and the missionary tour guides asked if anyone in her group felt anything—a strong emotion, a particular thought, even a "burning in their bosom." Jenny did. It was very strong and had begun just as she stepped onto the Temple grounds. When she returned home from vacation, she talked to some Mormon friends about what to do next. Sometime later, she was baptized. It was the best decision of her life.

Still, it has been more than a year and a half and she has yet to share in a meeting. The older women told her that it is not enough to *want* to share. It must be something more, a prompting or stirring from the Spirit. This time she has already felt it—a testimony from Heavenly Father. Perhaps it is strong this time because she is fasting, doing without food and water for a day just like all the other Saints. One of her friends made her laugh when she joked that it is a law of physics that time slows down in proportion to how long you go without food. It seemed that way this time. But then she felt that special knowing and was glad she had obeyed.

Every time she has sat in the chapel with her brothers and sisters, all doing without food and water and giving the money they save to the poor, she has felt a sense of belonging that nearly makes her weep. She knows she is part of something holy and eternal. She never knew anything like it outside in the sectarian church.

Now the testimonies are beginning. All throughout the chapel mothers keep their children in check and fathers listen carefully to what is said. They are the priesthood and must discern the hearts of everyone who shares. Jenny listens to that sweet Miss Garfield, nearly eighty, and to eight-year-old Tommy Dane, and to those two handsome missionaries just back from the field. What miracles they've seen! Heavenly Father has proven himself once again.

It is her turn. She stands, walks to the appointed place, and looks fully into the faces she loves so much. She says something light and humorous to ease her nervousness, something about only being nineteen and about how everyone probably thought she had done something wrong since she has never shared. The kind faces and smattering of laughter settle her. Then she says what she has been eager to say, what she has heard so many hundreds before proclaim. It is what Heavenly Father has given her a certainty about: "I know that Joseph Smith is the true Prophet of God and that he restored the true gospel. I know the Church of Jesus Christ of Latter-day Saints is the only true Church. I believe the Book of Mormon to be the true word of God. I believe that President Robert S. Monson is the only true Prophet upon the earth. I have this testimony from Heavenly Father."

Jenny sweeps her eyes around the room and sees the satisfaction in each face. She feels their acceptance. She wants to go further. Then a phrase comes to her. She's not sure where she first heard it but she remembers that it felt so confident, so certain about spiritual things. The Spirit must be giving her the words: "In fact, I want to say that without a doubt, I know as Thomas knew."

It was the strongest thing she knew to say. Just as the apostle Thomas had put his hands in the scars of Jesus to become certain that the Son of God was raised from the dead, Jenny is certain by the impression of the Spirit that what she has said is true: Joseph Smith was who he said he was. Everything he proclaimed was true. The Book of Mormon, the Church, and the true Prophet living today—Jenny has testimony of it all. And now she has given that testimony among the Saints. It is a holy thing. She isn't sure what she sees on the faces of the people. Perhaps they are proud of her. She hopes so. But she has affirmed the greatest truth she knows to the people she loves the most: "Joseph Smith is the greatest man who ever lived."

If the Church of Jesus Christ of Latter-day Saints should last a millennium and a half beyond the century and a half it has already known, it will still be wrestling with Joseph Smith. It would certainly prefer otherwise. Heavenly Father's eternal business is what the Church really wants to be about. The Saints do not really understand why the restoration of priesthood authority and the miracles of their history and the fruit of their way of living have not already proven themselves to the world.

Their frustration is natural but so is the incredulity of outsiders. Joseph Smith himself said he was a "rough stone rolling" and it was among the most prophetic statements he ever made. He has continued to roll roughly, unhewn and stonelike, through history—prophet and polygamist, deliverer and deceiver, visionary and vagabond, liberator and lecher—

certainly among the most unusual founders of a religion in the history of humanity.

He was born on December 23, 1805. It was the year Thomas Jefferson became president of the United States and then sent Meriwether Lewis and William Clark on an expedition to uncover the wonders of the continent. The infant nation was fighting its first war, not against the British as many Americans today suppose but against Islamic regimes on Africa's Barbary Coast. The French aristocrat Alexis de Tocqueville, the abolitionist William Lloyd Garrison, and the Danish weaver of fairy tales Hans Christian Andersen were all born the same year.

Smith began his life in Sharon, Vermont, but he spent his formative years near Palmyra, New York. It determined much of what he became. The region was famously labeled the "burned-over district" because there had been repeated waves of religious revivals that left many saved and rejoicing but more than a few cynical and weary of conventional religion. It helps to think of this area in the early 1800s as being something like California in the last half of the 1900s. It was strategic. It was a stretch of land 350 miles long and 25 miles wide that enveloped the primary carriage path connecting New England with the rest of the colonies. That primitive road took the approximate course that Highway 20 takes today. The region was also fertile. The new American government had forced the Iroquois natives out of the area largely to punish them for supporting the British during the Revolutionary War. This left acres of rich, unoccupied farmland for eager settlers to acquire.

Like the California of the next century, the burned-over district was also a land of exotic spirituality and religious experimentation. Some said it was because the Iroquois had attracted the attention of spirits who now claimed the sacred ground for their own. Others said that the region was particularly "thin," meaning that it was easy there to move beyond the physical and make contact with the supernatural.

Whatever its invisible qualities, the area drew religious rebels and innovators in droves. Among the more famous was Isaac Bullard. Wearing nothing but bearskin and beard, Bullard let his wooden "Prophet's Staff" decide where he went each day and where—if the stick suddenly stood on its end—his "Pilgrims" should build a church. There was also Mother Ann Lee, founder of the Shakers, who thought she was the reincarnation of Jesus Christ. Jemima Wilkinson, better known as "The Universal Friend," also thought she was Jesus Christ and ruled a community in Jerusalem—the one twenty-five miles from Joseph Smith's home. More mainstream were William Miller's Seventh Day Adventists. Then there were the attempts at "biblical communism" like the Oneida Community of John Humphrey Noyes. These and dozens of other spiritual novelties sprang from the burned-over district's mystically fertile soil.

Movements and religious communities were not the only measure of the region's power. There was also the bizarre brand of spirituality that individuals fashioned for themselves. As of 1800, barely 20 percent of the nation attended church. Then the evangelical revivals arose. Thousands were converted but rarely rooted in doctrine or mentored by a church. The newly awakened were left to do religion on their own, to craft a spirituality that conformed to their daily experience with nature and their superstitious understanding of the forces governing the world. This meant that despite the deeply Christian and sometimes transforming nature of the revivals, the religious worldview of many New England settlers afterward was an eclectic blend of magic, superstition, religious folklore, Native American spiritualism, and misapplied phrases from the King James Bible.

In short, the burned-over district became an occult buffet. Men used divining rods to find water and "seer stones" to find lost cattle. Symbols, amulets, tokens, and shapes gave a person some control over the spirits around him. The initiated understood that the stage of the moon guided everything from fence building to baby making. How a bird landed on a windowsill and which way a dog was facing when he barked became important matters to know. Spirits spoke through crackling fires and the afterbirth of a cow, were blocked in their evil intent by rituals, sayings, gestures, and vigilance. Men bound themselves together as well-meaning brothers through handshakes and secret garments, harmed each other with incantations and a dozen varieties of the evil eye. It became normal for a family to worship Jesus Christ with a Martin Luther hymn on a Sunday morning but then to read fortunes in ashes on Monday and pay diviners to walk their property at midweek.

Smith's family was typical of their time, their region, and the prevailing divinity. They were hardworking, untethered, and deeply mystical. His mother, Lucy, had witnessed scenes that might have driven others insane. A sister, Lovisa Mack, had once been near death from tuberculosis and laid in a coma for days. Then, without warning, the woman sat up suddenly, announced that Jesus Christ had healed her, asked her family to gently tug on her feet that she might be well—and she was! Lovisa became something of a celebrity in the area; she later claimed an open vision of Jesus and testified to her "miraculous recovery" for the rest of her life. Not long after, another sister, Lovina, also contracted tuberculosis. Lucy nursed her night and day. Finally, sensing the end, Lovina gathered her family and bid them farewell: "I'm going to rest—prepare to follow me."[2] She then sang a hymn, closed her eyes, folded her hands, and died. The deathbed charge sent Lucy into a season of guilt, prayer, Bible study, and tears that still left unanswered for her the great question of the age: "Which church is the right one to join?"

Not long after, Lucy met Joseph Smith, future father of the Prophet, a man of big dreams, small ability, spiritual wanderlust, and perpetual impoverishment. When the couple married, they owned a handsome farm and a reserve of cash. By the time

Joseph Jr. was born six years later, his father had already lost everything in a scheme to ship ginseng from China. This led to years of wandering small New England villages in search of work and escape from debts. Some of this work involved digging for buried treasure, which Joseph Sr. believed he could locate with a "hazel rod"—a forked stick by which Smith spiritually discerned hidden things. He also used seer stones—rocks that revealed secrets when the right man stared at them—and discerned their message best by putting them in a hat and then putting his face in the hat afterward. Like most of his neighbors, he saw no conflict between this mystical practice and his informal brand of Christianity. He believed in the Lord Jesus Christ and witches, in the God of the Bible and in spirits that lived in the ground. It was all equally true to him, and since he claimed to have discerned these mysteries he was often hired to find water and buried treasure with his divining fork, the upper end of which, he told people, "was attracted to money."[3]

Mention of the elder Smith's treasure hunting is usually trotted out to smear both his famous son and the religion he founded. It is no defense of either to say that being a "Money Digger" was common in that day. Rumors swirled throughout New England about how the Iroquois had buried riches years before and how white men with "the gift" had become wealthy by discerning and digging. The *Palmyra Herald* of July 24, 1822, reported, "at least five hundred respectable men . . . verily believe that immense treasures lie concealed upon our Green Mountains; many of whom have been for a number of years, most industriously and perseveringly engaged in digging it up. Some of them have succeeded beyond their most sanguine expectations."[4] It was odd by modern standards; it carried men into what are seen today as occult practices. But it was, in that day and for that region, quite normal.

None of it proved of value in lifting the Smith family's poverty and humiliation. Both would haunt Joseph Jr.'s early days. By the time he was five, the Smiths had moved three times. It must have seemed that sometimes even God was against them. Young Joseph would see a June in which snow fell and decimated crops. It would live in Vermont folklore as "eighteen-hundred-and-froze-to-death." It forced Joseph Sr. to leave the family to look for work. Not long after, the boy had to watch his mother load the wagon with the family's meager belongings, argue with creditors, and at one point physically grab the reins of her wagon out of the hands of a thieving teamster. Joseph was knocked down by one of this teamster's sons and left dazed and bleeding in the snow until a kind soul happened by and carried him to safety. Lucy and her children finally joined Joseph Sr. after a month of travel and with only two cents left to spare.

What Joseph's parents lacked in land and money they made up for in spiritual experiences and religious opinions. Lucy had once nearly died of a fever and begged and pleaded that God might spare her so she could raise her children. As she wrote years later in her memoir, *History of Joseph Smith by His Mother*, "I made a solemn covenant with God that if He would let me live I would endeavor to serve Him according to the best of my abilities. Shortly after this, I heard a voice say to me, 'Seek, and ye shall find; knock and it shall be opened unto you. Let your heart be comforted; ye believe in God, believe also in me.'" Lucy's health was restored and she began doing as she was told: seeking. She met only with disappointment, though—in ministers, in church doctrines, in denominations—and concluded at last "there was not then upon the earth the religion which I sought."

By a different route, her husband came to the same view. As Lucy recounted in her memoir, in 1811 Joseph Sr. was caught up in the religious excitement sweeping the region and it stirred in him anxiety about the "confusion and discord" among the Christian churches. He had a dream, the first of seven, which shaped his thinking about all religion. It is worth repeating here in full, given what was to come in the life of his son.

> I seemed to be traveling in an open, barren field, and as I was traveling, I turned my eyes towards the east, the west, the north and the south, but could see nothing save dead, fallen timber. Not a vestige of life, either animal or vegetable, could be seen; besides to render the scene still more dreary, the most death-like silence prevailed, no sound of anything animate could be heard in all the field.

I was alone in this gloomy desert, with the exception of an attendant spirit, who kept constantly by my side. Of him I inquired the meaning of what I saw, and why I was thus traveling in such a dismal place. He answered thus: "This field is the world, which now lieth inanimate and dumb, in regard to the true religion, or plan of salvation; but travel on, and by the wayside you will find on a certain log a box, the contents of which, if you eat thereof, will make you wise, and give unto you wisdom and understanding."

I carefully observed what was told me by my guide, and proceeding a short distance, I came to the box. I immediately took it up, and placed it under my left arm; then with eagerness I raised the lid, and began to taste of its contents; upon which all manner of beasts, horned cattle, and roaring animals, rose up on every side in the most threatening manner possible, tearing the earth, tossing their horns, and bellowing most terrifically all around me, and they finally came so close upon me, that I was compelled to drop the box and fly for my life. Yet, in the midst of all this I was perfectly happy, though I awoke trembling.

From this near apocalyptic dream, Joseph Sr. concluded "that there was no order or class of religionists that knew any more concerning the Kingdom of God than those of the world, or such as made no profession of religion whatever."[5]

We should remember that Lucy's account of her husband's dreams and her own spiritual encounters came years after they occurred, when she was pressed to explain the prophetic declarations of her infamous son. To some historians this compromises all that she claimed. Still, we can see in Lucy's remembrance the spiritual furniture of the Prophet Joseph Smith's early years: dreams and visions, the search for a "true gospel," spirit guides, revelations contained in objects, the certainty that Christianity had gone astray, special knowledge yet to be unveiled, the promise of a spiritual kingdom accessible to all willing to receive.

The Smith family's unending battle with poverty and their fierce spirituality are most of what we know of Joseph Smith's early life. There is little else available to us but the broad remembrances of later years. We do know that he was a good-looking child, who grew into a handsome man. He had a mystical turn of mind, which is no surprise given the age, the region, and the family in which he was raised. He had little education because of the Smiths' wanderings and want, but he was bright. He may also have been a bit of a prig. He said later that in his youth, he "fell into many vices and follies." We might expect tales of drunkenness, prostitutes, and theft. But no. Smith explained that he meant only that he "often had occasion to lament . . . a light, and too often vain mind, exhibiting a foolish and trifling conversation." We are almost disappointed.

Lucy recounts one of the few stories that survive from her son's pre-Prophet years in such a dramatic, overdone fashion that it is nearly too much to believe. It is true at its core, though, and even the theatrical retelling helps us see something of how both mother and son may have wished for the Prophet to be perceived.

In 1812 and 1813, typhoid fever tore through New England, killing 6,400 people in five months. In the Smith home, every one of the children fell ill. Sophronia, Joseph's younger sister, lay deadly still for nearly ninety days. She was entirely motionless for so long that once her parents thought she had died. When Lucy picked the girl's body up in a blanket to carry her to her grave, Sophronia breathed in and sobbed. Mercifully, she and all her siblings lived.

The fever left Joseph after two weeks. There seemed no reason for concern. Soon, though, he felt excruciating pain in his armpit. A doctor wrongly diagnosed it as a sprain. The pain continued for two weeks. The doctor returned, realized there was a fever sore under Joseph's arm, and lanced it. A quart of bilious liquid poured out. There was relief for a time but then the boy complained of pain in his leg. It too lasted for weeks and was nearly unbearable. Hyrum, Joseph's older brother, sat with him by the hour, Lucy recalled, "holding the affected part of his leg in his hands, and pressing it between them, so that his afflicted brother might be enabled to endure the pain."

We can feel compassion for a child's suffering but this is where Lucy's account begins to sound like overacted Victorian theater.

This is Joseph speaking to Joseph Sr., "Oh father! The pain is so severe, how can I bear it?"

Three weeks go by. Finally, a surgeon makes an eight-inch incision on the front side of the left leg between the knee and the ankle. There is relief but the pain continues and the surgeon cuts again, enlarging the wound "even to the bone."

Still, the leg grows worse and the family calls in "a council of surgeons."

"They being seated," Lucy writes, "I addressed them thus: 'Gentlemen, what can you do to save my boy's leg?'" The doctors say they must amputate but Lucy objects and proposes instead cutting out the diseased portion of the leg. The doctors relent.

It is difficult to believe that the Smiths had the means of summoning a "council of surgeons" or that if they did the learned men listened to an uneducated laborer's wife tell them to "cut out the diseased portion." But there is more drama to unfold.

As the doctors approach Joseph's bed, one of them says, "My poor boy, we have come again."

"Yes," says the valiant child. "I see you have; but you have not come to take off my leg, have you, sir?"

"No," replies the surgeon, "it is your mother's request that we make one more effort, and that is what we have now come for."

The doctor offers to bind Joseph to the bed.

"No, doctor. I will not be bound, for I can bear the operation much better if I have my liberty."

"Will you take some wine?" the doctor asks. "You must take something or you can never endure the severe operation to which you must be subjected."

"No," the seven-year-old replies. "I will not touch one particle of liquor, neither will I be tied down; but I will tell you what I will do—I will have my father sit on the bed and hold me in his arms and then I will do whatever is necessary in order to have the bone taken out."

Then, this is Joseph speaking to Lucy: "Mother, I want you to leave the room, for I know you cannot bear to see me suffer so; father can stand it, but you have carried me so much, and watched over me so long, you are almost worn out." His eyes began filling with tears. "Now, mother promise me that you will not stay, will you? The Lord will help me, and I shall get through with it."

It is the sweet remembrance of a sixty-nine-year-old mother writing of her son's surgery thirty years after it occurred. Perhaps it is natural that the memory should be reworked into a hero tale. However, it is disappointing that this overblown recollection has become a fact in the minds of the faithful. More engaging would have been the likely truth:

a scared child, a tearful mother, surgeons doing their best, and all surviving a horrific experience.

What followed were months of agonizing recovery. Pieces of bone missed by the surgeon later worked their way to the surface. Lucy or one of her other sons carried the weakened Joseph wherever he needed to go. When the boy was strong enough, he was sent to the home of an uncle who lived by the sea, where he spent many more months healing. Full recovery took a year, and Smith still walked with a distinctive limp for the rest of his life.

Years passed. There was the War of 1812 and the year of the June snow and the family's move to Palmyra, New York. Always there were swirling revivals and religious upheavals. Stories of healings and visions filled tavern chatter. Jesus was busy. He appeared to dozens, hundreds, in a variety of garb with contradictory instructions for the church. It was, to the Smiths, a troubling, cynical time that confirmed their unshakable beliefs: the Christian church was lost, there was a true gospel yet to be revealed, and meanwhile the world lay in unendurable darkness.

To Americans hearing the Mormon story through the years, the spiritual landscape of the burned-over district has probably felt like familiar territory. It is the United States in microcosm. The entire religious history of the country has had the feel of those square miles of New England in the early 1800s: a new spiritual frontier pioneered by bold experimenters who blended together disparate mystical and theological cultures in hopes of something new. As in that overheated district, churches have always fought. In every generation, well-intentioned people have made widely differing claims. Confusion has often reigned.

That the Mormons present themselves as the solution for a burned-over culture has only helped them in appealing to a religiously "burned-over" nation. They grew out of religious weariness. They found solutions no else had. They understand how pitiful it all seems. Join them, and break from the madness. This is one of the most appealing aspects of the Mormon Church for Americans today, and it is a narrative that grows organically and compellingly from the Joseph Smith story.

CHAPTER 3

JOSEPH SMITH: PROPHET AND MAGICIAN

Now, most historians, Mormon or not, who work with the sources, accept as fact Joseph Smith's career as village magician. Too many of his closest friends and family admitted as much, and some of Joseph's own revelations support the contention.[1]

—Marvin S. Hill, LDS historian

"Dr. Felder, we can't psychologize everything. It turns us all into bad Sigmund Freuds!"

"Mr. Taylor, I know it is difficult for you to hear, but if you are going to become a historian of any merit, you must lay aside your religious brainwashing to consider this most obvious of truths. Joseph Smith's entire religion was rooted in hatred of his father. For God's sake, a freshman psychology major could see it!"

"That's crazy! He loved his father! He had him witness the plates and even made him a patriarch. I don't object to what you're saying because I'm a Mormon. I object because you couldn't be more wrong on the basis of the evidence! You're letting a secular bias blind you."

"Easy, young man. First, don't assume you know anything about how secular I am. You're simply not qualified to comment on the soul of a Jew. But more to the point: Joseph Smith ought to be renamed Oedipus. That's how clear the case is."

"Not that again! I suppose he had problems potty training too?"

"Listen and learn, Mr. Taylor. Smith's father put the family through hell. No money. Creditors always in pursuit. Ever relocating. Nothing a boy could be proud of in his father. Do you remember that Lucy, the mother, used to read a book of her own father's heroic exploits to her children? What would that produce but a sense of shame for the father by comparison to the grandfather? The distinction would not have been lost on a bright lad like our Joseph. The conflict in his soul is obvious in later years. In his memoirs, Smith states that his father was poor so frequently it is as though he is trying to exorcise his feelings. Then, in Fawn Brodie's biography, she mentions that young Smith was insolent to his father early on. What does this mean to you? Finally, we have the boastful statement from Smith that he brought salvation to his father's house. This he proclaimed repeatedly. Now, surely you can see the scarlet thread?"

"Dr. Felder, each of those facts is true, but it doesn't make for the dark picture you paint. I mean, most of those things could be said of me, after all!"

"Don't make that mistake, Mr. Taylor. You know better. And let me close the matter with words from one of your own sainted historians. I can do no better in your eyes, no? Let us see, where is it? Ah, yes. Your Richard Lyman Bushman—I believe you know the name—wrote, "If there was any childhood dynamic at work in Joseph Jr.'s life, it was the desire to redeem his flawed, loving father."[2]

"Now come on, Dr. Felder! You didn't finish the quote. The question that comes after the word *father* is, 'but was this enough to make him a prophet?' Bushman was questioning the very approach you are taking. The question was, 'Could pain alone make a man a prophet?'"

"And that is the question indeed, isn't it, Mr. Taylor? Perhaps it is enough that one of your Latter-day historians—a fellow Harvard man, no less—is willing to consider the question at all. But here is the more critical question for you: Did Joseph Smith create a religion centered upon a Heavenly Father to compensate for the shame he felt about his earthly father?"

For the faithful, what began to unfold in the middle of Joseph Smith's teenage years was in keeping with the grand scheme of revelation. It was natural, logical—indeed, obvious—that young Joseph Smith was being divinely prepared for a mission from God. For the more secular, more wary psychologist or historian, it is not obvious at all. Smith was not a chosen one so much as one marred—marred by the ravages of his tumultuous childhood. There was the instability of his family home with its constant moves, haunting want, humiliating debts, and spirit of failure. There was a sensitive child likely scarred in every way by fever, unspeakably painful surgeries, a year of recovery, and a lasting limp. And there was the ever-present spiritual world— ever intruding in dreams and impressions, ever murky as to intent, ever definitive about its displeasure and ever promising revelation that had yet to come.

Either calling or torment, then, moved Smith to fear for his soul in the middle of his second decade of life. He remembered later that at about the age of twelve until about the age of fifteen, he "pondered many things in my heart concerning the situation of the world . . . and the darkness which pervaded the minds of mankind—my mind became exceedingly distressed for I became convicted of my sins."[3] In search of relief he scoured the Bible and gave himself to nights of prayer. These seem rather serious reflections for a fifteen-year-old boy, but perhaps they were typical in that time.

Finally, the oft-told story goes, Smith was driven by spiritual hunger and the religious strife that surrounded him to seek his God. This is why, in the spring of 1820, he walked into the woods and knelt in a grove to pray. Since what happened next is the beginning of the Mormon faith, we should allow Smith to speak unedited in his own voice.

It was the first time in my life that I had made such an attempt, for amidst all my anxieties I had never as yet made the attempt to pray vocally. . . . I kneeled down and began to offer up the desires of my heart to God. I had scarcely done so, when immediately I was seized upon by some power which entirely overcame me, and had such an astonishing influence over me as to bind my tongue so that I could not speak. Thick darkness gathered around me, and it seemed to me for a time as if I were doomed to sudden destruction. But, exerting all my powers to call upon God to deliver me out of the power of this enemy which had seized upon me, and at the very moment when I was ready to sink into despair and abandoned myself to destruction—not to an imaginary ruin, but to the power of some actual being from the unseen world, who had such marvelous power as I had never felt in any being—just at this moment of great alarm, I saw a pillar of light exactly over my head, above the brightness of the sun, which descended gradually until it fell upon me.

It no sooner appeared than I found myself delivered from the enemy which held me bound. When the light rested upon me I saw two personages, whose brightness and glory defy all description, standing above me in the air. One of them spake unto me, calling me by name and said—pointing to the other—"This is my beloved Son, hear Him."

My object in going to inquire of the Lord was to know which of all the sects was right, that I might know which to join. No sooner, therefore, did I get possession of myself, so as to be able to speak, than I asked the personages who stood above me in the light, which of all the sects was right—and which I should join. I was answered that I must join none of them, for they were all wrong, and the personage who addressed me said that all their creeds were an abomination in His sight: that those professors were all corrupt; that "they draw near to me with their lips, but their hearts are far from me; they teach for doctrines the commandments of men: having a form of godliness, but they deny the power thereof." He again forbade me to join with any of them; and many other things did he say unto me which I cannot write at this time. When I came to myself again, I found myself lying on my back, looking up into heaven.[4]

This was how Smith recounted his experience—it has come to be known as the "First Vision"—in 1834, fourteen years after the event. He offered other versions and this has made non-LDS historians incredulous if not incensed, though it does not seem to disturb LDS scholars at all. In an account he gave in 1831 or 1832, he said that the vision came when he was sixteen and that "the Lord opened the heavens upon me and I saw the Lord." Then, in 1835, there were the two "personages" in a "pillar of fire" and with "many angels." These discrepancies may be the result of Smith unveiling a cherished experience bit by sacred bit over the years, but there is also the possibility that he imagined the tale more gloriously with each retelling.

He apparently did not tell his parents about the vision at first. Perhaps it was too precious or perhaps he thought they would not believe him. He did find himself in the presence of a Methodist minister soon after and decided to describe his experience to this man. There were two problems with this plan. First, not all ministers believed that visions and miracles and such continued to occur after the last of Jesus' disciples passed away. Smith had stumbled into the presence of one who did not. Second, even if the minister had believed miraculous experiences were possible, Smith's vision declared all Christianity corrupt and an abomination in the sight of God. He was naive to think that any minister would be grateful for what he had to share. The Methodist clergyman certainly wasn't. He told Smith his vision was from the devil, that God no longer gave such revelations, and then he repeated Smith's story all over town. Persecution and prejudice followed, which may have caused the fledgling prophet to keep to himself for a time. He farmed, he became skilled with the divining rod and the seer stone under his father's tutelage, and he pondered the meaning of what he had experienced. He was only fourteen years old.

The next day of destiny came on September 21, 1823. Joseph was seventeen. While praying in bed late in the evening, another visitation occurred. This time an angel appeared in the teenager's bedroom, clothed in "exquisite whiteness" and floating several inches above the floor. The spirit announced himself as "Moroni" and said he had a "work" for Joseph to do.

> He said there was a book deposited, written upon gold plates, giving an account of the former inhabitants of this continent and the source from whence they sprang. He also said that the fulness of the everlasting Gospel was contained in it, as delivered by the savior to the ancient inhabitants; Also, that there were two stones in silver bows—and these stones, fastened to a breastplate, constituted what is called the Urim and Thummim—deposited with the plates; and the possession and use of these stones were what constituted 'seers' in ancient or former times; and that God had prepared them for the purpose of translating the book.[5]

The angel then began to quote Scripture, though he altered the traditional words significantly. This stuck in the boy's mind. The angel also offered "many explanations which cannot be mentioned here," commanded Joseph not to show the plates to anyone, and then gave the boy a vision showing where these plates could be found.

With this, the angel ascended, only to reappear moments later and give exactly the same announcement, word for word. He added only a warning of great judgment and destruction to come upon the earth and then, once again, ascended.

Still, Moroni was not done. He let Joseph recover for a moment and then reappeared to warn the boy of covetousness and to say that he should not think the book on golden plates was for his own profit, that he should guard his mind against darkness, and, finally, that he should tell his father all he had been told.

The next day Joseph, his father, and his brother, Alvin, were working in the fields. Alvin noticed that Joseph had stopped moving and seemed to be in a trance. "We must not slacken our hands or we will not be able to complete our task!" Alvin yelled. Apparently, this was how field hands spoke in those days. Joseph returned to work but then stopped again, and this drew the attention of his father who saw he was pale and told him to go home. On the way, Joseph rested under an apple tree. And Moroni appeared yet again.

> "Why did you not tell your father that which I commanded you to tell him?"
>
> "I was afraid my father would not believe me," Joseph replied.
>
> "He will believe every word you say to him," the angel assured.[6]

Joseph promised that he would tell his father and then did. The elder Smith replied that Joseph should go and do exactly as commanded by the angel. Not long after, the boy went to the hill he had seen in the vision. It was the Hill Cumorah in Ontario County, New York, a few miles from the Smiths' house. There, he said he saw a great, rounded stone. He pried the stone out of his way, peered beneath and saw the plates, the Urim and the Thummim, and the breastplate just as the angel had said. The boy tried to take the articles with him but Moroni appeared again and stopped him. Joseph would have to return each year for four years before he could remove the plates from their place.

Joseph did as commanded. Each year on September 22, he returned and received from the angel "instruction and intelligence." He also told his family everything, repeating the angel's warning that no one else should be told. During these years, Lucy reported, Joseph prepared for the day he would take the plates by learning to keep the commandments of God.

It must have been difficult returning to life's routines after five visitations of an angel just three years after seeing God the Father and his Son. Smith had no choice, apparently, but it helped that he did not return only to his work in the fields.

A man named Stowell (Smith spelled it "Stoal" in his accounts) arrived at the Smith home just after all these supernatural events and asked to hire Joseph for digging up treasure on his Pennsylvania farm. It was not Joseph Sr. he came for. It was the son. Stowell had heard the boy "possessed certain keys, by which he could discern things invisible to the natural eye." It is confirmation of the testimony given by numerous witnesses in later years. Joseph Smith Jr. had a gift. He had learned from his father how to work the hazel fork or divining rod and he had become even more adept than his father at obtaining revelations from seer stones. He—like his father—saw what others could not see by peering into rocks. He too put his personal seer stones into a hat, put his face in after them, and told those who hired him where Indian treasures were buried or where water awaited a pump or where the Spanish had hidden their gold. His gift was strong. His reputation grew. Men from hundreds of miles away hired him.

In 1825, Joseph, his father, and several other diggers journeyed to Stowell's farm in the Susquehanna Valley and got to work. Later accounts said that the men fasted and prayed to break the "charm" protecting the treasure. Once they discerned the proper location, they sprinkled the blood of a lamb on the spot to satisfy the "spirit below."[7] Little came of it. They uncovered no treasure.

They did find trouble, though. One of Stowell's neighbors, Peter Bridgman, swore out a warrant for young Smith's arrest on the charge that he was a "disorderly person" and an "imposter." At the time, most states had laws against the kind of practices Smith used to recover treasure. The New York law stated that "disorderly persons" included "all jugglers (conjurors), and all persons pretending to have skill in physiognomy palmistry, or like crafty science, or pretending to tell fortunes, or to discover lost goods."[8] Clearly, this described Joseph Smith.

A trial ensued. The exact verdict of the court is lost to us. There were, though, two lasting results of the matter. First, Smith's defense amounted to numerous witnesses attesting that he was an astonishingly good diviner. Second, Smith was arrested for a crime and that crime had to do with an occult practice. Both served to delight Smith's critics and to tarnish his reputation for the rest of his life.

This episode has forced historians to deal with Smith's devotion to clairvoyance, magic, and astrology—however unwillingly. For those who doubt the existence of a supernatural realm, the matter is of little consequence. Smith's occultism is no different from the type of imagined revelations that created Mormonism to begin with. For traditional Christians and members of several other faiths—Islam, for example—the matter is vital, for it points to a possible source of Smith's heretical revelations other than what he claimed and other than mere human imagination. That other source is demonic spirits.

Fearing this very charge, there was a time when the Church would have denied Smith's occult practices. To its credit, it does so no longer. The evidence is too strong, the historical record too clear. Even the dean of LDS historians, Richard Lyman Bushman, in his definitive *Joseph Smith: Rough Stone*

Rolling, admits that the Smith family was primarily known in their region as treasure seekers, that they lived in a "culture of magic," that they were adept in the use of seer stones, and that they, like their neighbors, held "Christian belief in angels and devils blended with belief in guardian spirits and magical powers."[9]

Dissident LDS historian D. Michael Quinn takes this further. In his encyclopedic *Early Mormonism and the Magic World View*, Quinn documents that the Smith family owned "magical charms, divining rods, amulets, a ceremonial dagger inscribed with astrological symbols of Scorpio and seals of Mars, and parchments marked with occult signs."[10] Mitch Horowitz, author of the helpful and popular *Occult America: White House Séances, Ouija Circles, Masons, and the Secret Mystic History of Our Nation*, confirms that Joseph Smith "venerated the powers of the planet Jupiter" and even died with a silver amulet of Jupiter in his pocket. This devotion to charms and symbols may be what drew Smith to Freemasonry in later years. Even LDS historians admit that many of the Church's ceremonies were influenced by the Freemasonic worldview and rituals, as we shall see.

Leading Mormons have made peace with Smith's occultism by understanding it as "divine tutoring."[11] It was the way the Prophet was prepared for the revelatory experiences to come in his life, the means by which he was schooled in supernatural processes so he could endure the weight of a greater unveiling. Others, particularly evangelical Christians, view this as excuse making for a man who lived in harmony with evil spirits and who then made a magical worldview the basis of his new religion. Neither side is likely to convince the other, but it is significant that Joseph Smith never abandoned his trust in magical objects, incantations, and secret signs. He clung to his occult and Freemasonic associations even to the last day of his life. As he died in 1844, he formed his arms into a square and shouted, "Oh, Lord my God, is there no help for the widow's son!" It was a plea from a Mason for help from other Masons using signs and phrases all Masons knew.

Whatever aid Smith's devotion to magic and clairvoyance was to him, it did not help him win his wife. While digging treasure for Stowell, he boarded in the home of Isaac Hale and soon fell in love with Isaac's daughter Emma. She was an enigma of the kind that appealed to Joseph's bruised and mystical soul. She was dark haired and pretty and gave the impression of being shy. But she also had an active, eager mind that kept rule over a volcanic inner fire. Joseph would know its eruptions in later years, but in these earlier, more innocent days the hint of it must have awakened passion. On a trip home to keep his annual appointment with Moroni, Joseph told his mother that he wanted to marry Emma Hale.

The problem was Emma's father, Isaac. He was a hunter who earned his way honestly and he had no intention of giving his innocent daughter to an "imposter" who "followed a business I could not approve."[12] He meant money digging and water divining and gazing into stones. It all disgusted Hale and he could never let his daughter marry such a man.

He was in the minority, though. Joseph's mother encouraged the match. Even Stowell, Joseph's employer, urged the couple on. Stowell even invited Emma to visit his home so she could be closer to Joseph. This may have been a prearranged scheme. Both Stowell and Joseph pressured Emma and finally, overwhelmed, she agreed to marry Joseph in the home of a nearby squire. It was January 18, 1827. Afterward, the couple moved in with Joseph's parents. Emma wrote her father, told him of the marriage, and asked for her clothing and furniture if not his blessing. Isaac Hale told her the goods were hers but she and Joseph would have to return and claim them.

They did—and Joseph was fortunate he was not killed. Hale was furious. "You have stolen my daughter and married her," the man raged through his tears. "I had much rather have followed her to her grave. You spend your time in digging for money—pretend to see in a stone, and thus try to deceive people."

The sensitive Joseph wept, realizing what he had done. He swore never to "see in a stone" again and admitted that his reputation for mystical gifts with stones and rods was a pretense. He would not "peep" again. Appeased, Hale offered to help the couple get established in business, if only Joseph would show himself good to his word.

He wasn't. One evening after Joseph and Emma had returned to the Smiths' home, Joseph was late returning from business in the neighboring village. When he finally entered the house, his father pressed him about where he had been. Joseph smiled and replied, "I have taken the severest chastisement that I have ever had in my life." There are differing accounts of what followed. Some say Joseph Sr. assumed his son had misbehaved in some way and began to chastise him. This would have said something of the relationship between the two men. Other accounts have Joseph Sr. becoming angry that anyone would speak harshly to his boy. This is the version preferred by adoring mother, Lucy.

However Joseph Sr. responded, his son quickly set him straight. "Stop, Father, stop," the younger man protested, "it was the angel of the Lord: as I passed by the hill of Cumorah, where the plates are, the angel met me, and said that I had not been engaged enough in the work of the Lord; that the time had come for the Record to be brought forth; and that I must be up and doing, and set myself about the things which God had commanded me to do. But, Father, give yourself no uneasiness concerning the reprimand which I have received, for I know the course I am to pursue, so all will be well."

The family had some sense of what this meant. The appearance of Moroni and the visitation of the Heavenly Father and the Son had been much discussed and pondered. Every member of the Smith household knew that September 22, 1827, approached: the fourth anniversary of the promise of the plates. It was time for the "work" of Joseph Smith to begin. An "everlasting gospel" waited to be unearthed from a nearby hill. A new and divinely ordained era was about to begin.

The spiritual culture captured in the famous story of Joseph Smith, Moroni, and the plates is the spiritual culture of Mormonism. Men have certain spiritual gifts. Angels appear. Revelations come. Objects possess revelatory power. Symbols and signs are important. An anointed man tells others what God is about. The sacred is guarded by secrets.

What is not captured in the story is also revealing. There is no conversion experience. For years there is no revelation of what is true, merely revelation that all religions are wrong. There is no rebuke from the angel for Smith's use of the occult. Being in the presence of God does little to alter character. Always the outside world misunderstands and persecutes.

It is not surprising that this founding story has determined much of what Mormonism is today. It is a tale often told, usually in reverent tones, so that every part of the story imbeds itself in the soul of the Saint, reproducing its spirit and view of the world in each LDS generation. It is one example of why the power of story has defined Mormons more than any other force except perhaps their view of revelation. It is also why one of their presidents was right when he said, "Mormonism . . . must stand or fall on the story of Joseph Smith."

CHAPTER 4

THE GOLDEN PLATES

This book must be either true or false. If true, it is one of the most important messages ever sent from God to man. . . . If false, it is one of the most cunning, wicked, bold, deep-laid impositions ever palmed upon the world.[1]

—Orson Pratt, LDS Apostle

"Oh my goodness. That was . . . that was a trip! I feel like I need a shower!"

"What? What in the world do you mean?" This question comes from Ashley. She's a tall, thin black woman in her mid-twenties who reminds her friends of the singer Toni Braxton—except that Ashley can't sing and she dresses better.

"Listen, you *cannot*, I repeat, *cannot* sit and listen to a bunch of fools sing about 'F-ing' God and not get some of that on you." This is Jackie. She's known as the funny one but she's pretty too, and smart. She's just starting at a big firm uptown—the first black woman there ever!—even though the ink on her Georgetown diploma is still wet.

"Oh, no. Don't tell me you sat there for three hours and missed the whole point! Don't tell me!" Ashley's a bit of a scold. It comes naturally. She's a nurse practitioner at Mount Sinai.

"I did not miss the point! I got the point jammed right in my face!" Jackie can get loud. "And Virgil's is this way, by the way. I don't know where you think you're going." The two friends laugh knowingly, almost collapsing on each other. Ashley's always getting lost. They have just stepped out of the O'Neill Theatre where they've seen the play *The Book of Mormon*. Now, there's only one thing to do: get to the best hush puppies in New York—which are waiting just across Times Square at Virgil's Barbecue.

"I just can't believe I spent that kind of money to get slimed. You are definitely buying tonight."

"No I'm not. And I can't believe you didn't like it. It's your kind of thing! You know—sarcasm and satire and all that *Saturday Night Live* stuff you love so much."

"Satire I get. This play was blasphemy. I mean, it was just sacrilege!" Jackie shakes her head in disgust.

"Girl, when did you become a Mormon? Since when do you care what the South Park guys say about the Saints? Last time I checked you were AME." It's Ashley, scolding again.

"You know I am. But this thing wasn't just about Mormons. It was about religion. And it was *nasty*!"

"That was the whole point! They were trying to show how men just make up a bunch of crap and call it religion and then force it on everybody else. You remember that course we took at UVA? Sexton talked about that Feuerbach guy and how he said man creates religion just because he has an inner need for religion whether it's true or not? Remember? He was one of the dudes who influenced Marx." Ashley can't help herself. Lecturing is her second language.

"Of course I remember. I did better in that class than you." Jackie says this with a smile. Still, she's not backing down. "But, I mean, this thing, this play: it had people having sex with frogs and circumcising women and that General What's-His-Name naked. It was just more than this woman could take!"

"But didn't it touch you? Don't you see? They made up that nasty religion right there on stage to show how most religion gets made up in the first place—because somebody needs a religion to get made up. It's almost never about God. The missionaries were haunted by their 'Spooky Mormon Hell Dream'—that was awesome!—or some prideful thing about Orlando. The villagers just wanted to get away from their suffering by making it to the heavenly 'Saltlakecity.' And the whole point was that it didn't really matter what anyone believed. Religion was always about something else. I mean that one missionary hadn't even read the book he was supposed to be preaching! It was perfect!"

"Yeah, I guess. I guess they were making a point. It was just too much—like drinking from a fire hose." Jackie goes quiet for a moment, realizing she may have missed something important about the play.

Ashley has not gone quiet. She's become a little indignant. "Well, not everybody had a great church and a great pastor and great family like you, Jackie. Some of us got pretty messed up in screwy religions. You know I barely got out of all that."

"I know. I didn't mean—"

"I know. I know. No worries." Ashley gentles up. "But it just felt good to have someone saying, 'You know, sometimes they pull this stuff out of their ear. Sometimes it's as much a bad joke as you think it is.' I guess that's why I couldn't stop the laughing or the tears."

"All right. I see what you mean. Here. Let's talk about it over some snacks." The two arrive at Virgil's, the smell of wood smoke and maple drawing them in. Just inside the door, Jackie comes to a full stop. She's just remembered: "But you're going to have to pray for me before we eat so I'm not thinking about those maggots they kept talking about on that stage. Lord, I wish I'd never heard that!"

Among the challenges Mormons face in winning Americans to their faith is that the story behind their Book of Mormon is all too—human. The Judeo-Christian legacy that has defined American culture has also set expectations about revelation. The LDS version seems to break all the rules.

To a people influenced by the worldview of the Bible, revelation comes as the final word to a man who is changed by the experience and this word is repeatedly confirmed by the course of events thereafter. There is no missing the smoking mountain, stone tablets, earthquake, and finger of God attending the revelation to Moses on Mount Sinai. Abraham was so certain of his revelation that he nearly killed his own son trying to obey. Ezekiel saw the spinning wheels, great throne, glory cloud, heavenly commotion, and attending angels of God—one scholar calls it "God's motor home"—and then accurately predicted events in his own time and times that had not yet begun. Men might have complained to God (Habakkuk), argued with God (David), tried to run from God (Jonah), and even tried to sue God (Job), but always the revelation they received was final, the man was forever changed, and the God who spoke confirmed his words again and again. It is why the tablets of Moses traveled with wandering Israel—as unceasing testimony that God had spoken to his people once and for all.

In the New Testament, voices sounded from heaven, the ground shook, lights flashed, and people thought lightning had sounded when God spoke. The earthly Messiah met with his Heavenly Father and his entire body radiated blinding light. Men were guided in writing scripture, yet in such a way that their times and personalities left an imprint on the page. So great is God. Sometimes revelation was not a "showing of" but a "taking to." The apostle John ended up in the throne room of God on the Lord's Day. The apostle Paul ended up in the Third Heaven. Those who dared to deceive or oppose such men ended up dead.

If God did not quite behave as Cecil B. DeMille's movie *The Ten Commandments* seems to indicate he should, he also did not behave as though he was playing George Burns or Morgan Freeman. And he certainly rose above the Boomer God of *Field of Dreams*. God's presence transformed, holiness resulted, there were ethical demands, every syllable was tirelessly preserved, and the God who spoke was the same God who had spoken the universes into being.

The Mormon tale is different, as we've seen. Revelation comes first to a fourteen-year-old. He is visited by God and his Son. Nothing happens after they leave. Then, sometime later, an angel—who was once a man—appears in that same teenager's bedroom. Apparently the angel or his God are so unsure about this lad that the angelic being not only reappears five times in twenty-four hours—three times to deliver exactly the same message—but then tells the boy he is not ready to proceed and will have to wait four years. He is also warned that the whole purpose of the revelation is not to make him rich. Apparently there was some question about this. In the meantime, the boy farms, digs ditches, and makes a living in the occult.

Then comes what we are about to see unfold. When the time for the revelation arrives, the boy is not supposed to tell anyone. Even those who assist him cannot see the plates upon which the revelation is given. The young man "translates" the plates in exactly the way he used to hunt for hidden water and buried treasure—his face jammed into his hat while he stares at stones. It is the same practice for which he has been arrested years before.

Actually, the word *translate* does not apply because even the boy does not claim to understand the language in which the plates are written. Their meaning must come by revelation. This brings, of course, the whole purpose of the plates into question from the start. During the process of this translation, an angry wife steals, sells, or destroys some of the translated work. It is never recovered. Neighbors try to run off with it. Years later, sworn witnesses will become unsure about what they've seen, then become sure again, then claim they saw the plates in a vision, and then swear again that they've seen the plates however that "seeing" may have occurred. Most of those involved in the early story will not think much of the adult version of the young man and will not be friends with him by the end of his life.

There is more. The revelation will become a book and it will create quite a stir. Yet the movement it spawns will not be controversial primarily for what the book contains. It will be far more controversial for revelations that come later, some of which directly contradict the book's teachings. The historical claims of the book will almost never receive scholarly affirmation outside of the faithful fold, but this will mean little to the faithful themselves despite the fact that many of them are well-educated people who are leaders in their professions.

It is, in short, one of the most unusual tales of revelation in human history. And it all began with Joseph Smith, who, when we left him at the end of the last chapter, was married to Emma, trying to convince his father-in-law he wasn't a nut, having annual meetings with the angel Moroni, and eagerly awaiting September 22, 1827, for his divine calling to commence.

Finally, the appointed day came and Joseph Smith returned to the Hill Cumorah and received the prophesied plates from Moroni. He was warned not to be irresponsible with them or he would be "cut off." He was also told not to let anyone see them. He carried them into his parents' house after midnight, showed the Urim and the Thummim—a type of spectacles with seer stones for lenses—to his mother, and then locked everything away in a chest.

In the official version of his story that would later appear in the Church's *Pearl of Great Price*, Smith described the gold plates as being "six inches wide and eight inches long and not quite so thick as a common tin. They were filled with engravings, in Egyptian characters and bound together in a volume, as the leaves of a book with three rings running through the whole." The Urim and the Thummim—historically the name of a decision-making device used by priests in ancient Israel—Smith said were "two transparent stones set in the rim of a bow fastened to a breastplate." And so, he proclaims simply, "through the medium of the Urim and Thummim I translated the record by the gift, and power of God."

The big and pressing question is whether these plates ever even existed. A small circle around Smith said they did and this testimony is what Mormons today place their trust in. Emma Smith was her husband's first scribe and she remembered how she "wrote day after day, often sitting at the table close by him, he sitting with his face buried in his hat with the stone in it." Meanwhile, "the plates often lay on the table without any attempt at concealment."[2] A schoolteacher named Oliver Cowdery also helped and later said, "To sit under the sound of a voice dictated by the inspiration of heaven, awakened the utmost gratitude of this bosom!"

Oddly, Cowdery once asked to do some of the translating himself, meaning that he wanted to look through the seer stones and read the original words of the language Smith had named "Reformed Egyptian." Smith sought a revelation about the matter and received one. Heavenly Father agreed, but when Cowdery tried to see what Smith could see through the stones and the hat, he failed. Obviously, the holy work of translating was Smith's alone. Or, perhaps Cowdery could see nothing in the stones because Smith was a fraud manipulating even his own wife into believing he was hearing from God.

A man named David Whitmer visited Smith during this time and reported "Joseph Smith would put the seer stone into a hat, and put his face in the hat. . . . One character at a time would appear, and under it was the interpretation in English. Thus, the Book of Mormon was translated by the gift and power of God, and not by any power of man."[3]

Perhaps the weirdest episode of all involved one of Smith's financiers, Martin Harris, who was notoriously gullible, perhaps simpleminded, and addicted to the mystical claims of more confident men. He too served as Smith's scribe and this only angered his wife, who was tired of her husband's time and money going to Joseph Smith. Harris begged Smith to let him take some of the manuscript home to show his wife and calm her down. Smith refused. Harris begged again. Smith had a revelation and decided to let the man take the complete translation—by June 1828 it was just over a hundred pages—to the enraged woman.

It was a mistake but Smith was distracted. Emma had just given birth to a boy who lived only a few hours and it had been such a traumatic delivery that Emma was near death too. Joseph tended her until she improved. When he turned his attention to translating again, he discovered that Harris's wife had stolen the sacred pages.

They were never found. Harris wept and apologized. Smith thought all was lost until he had another revelation, the angel declaring God "will only cause thee to be afflicted for a season, and thou art still chosen, and wilt again be called to the work." The translating resumed. Smith was told—again by a convenient revelation—that he should not retranslate the 116 missing pages since the devil would make sure that the stolen pages were translated in altered form to discredit Smith's revelatory work. However, God had a plan. He'd seen this coming. He had another book for Smith to translate and it would cover the same period as the earlier pages but would take a different approach. This brought the book of Nephi into the manuscript and also allowed Smith to pick up his work, presumably, at page 117. Heavenly Father was always there for Joseph Smith.

The pressing question is whether Joseph Smith's plates actually existed or whether they were a part of—in the words of an early Mormon leader—"one of the most cunning, wicked, bold, deep-laid impositions ever palmed upon the world."[4]

Smith's father-in-law certainly thought the latter: "I conscientiously believe ... that the whole 'Book of Mormon' (so called) is a silly fabrication of falsehood and wickedness, got up for speculation, and with design to dupe the credulous and unwary—and in order that its fabricators might live upon the spoils of those who swallowed the deception."[5]

Eminent historian Fawn M. Brodie also thought that Smith invented the whole tale—and then in time came to believe his own deception. Brodie was a gifted scholar, the first woman to receive tenure in the history department at UCLA, and was celebrated for her biographies of Smith, Thomas Jefferson, and Richard Nixon, among others. She is a controversial figure in LDS history because, though she was raised in a leading Mormon family—she was the niece of David O. McKay, an LDS president—she wrote *No Man Knows My History: The Life of Joseph Smith*, in which she concluded that the founder of Mormonism was a "genius of improvisation."

In her book, Brodie cited a conversation Smith supposedly had with a man named Peter Ingersoll, a conversation she admits was "savagely cynical." According to Ingersoll, the entire lie of the angel, the golden plates, and the Book of Mormon started one day when Smith had tied some white sand into his shirt. When he took it home and his family asked what he was carrying, he played a cruel joke. Ingersoll remembered Smith saying:

> At the moment I happened to think of what I had heard about a history found in Canada, called the golden Bible; so I very gravely told them it was the golden Bible. To my surprise, they were credulous enough to believe what I said. Accordingly, I told them that I had received a commandment to let no one see it, for, says I, no man can see it with the naked eye and live. However, I offered to take out the book and show it to them, but they refused to see it, and left the room. Now, I have got the damned fools fixed and will carry out the fun.[6]

Ingersoll also remembered that Smith "told me he had no such book, and believed there never was any such book." Yet, to deceive his family and the naive, Smith "made a box . . . of clapboards, and put it into a pillow case, and allowed people only to lift it, and feel of it through the case."[7]

Another Smith acquaintance reported that the whole deception began as an attempt on Smith's part to manipulate this acquaintance into building a chest. The man refused, and, "A few days afterward, he told one of my neighbors that he had not got any such book, nor never had such an one; but that he had told the story to deceive the d—d fool, (meaning me,) to get him to make a chest."[8]

For recounting these recollections in her book and for making the case that Smith cynically invented the revelations that became Mormonism, Brodie was criticized by the Church but honored by non-LDS scholars and reviewers. In 1946, the Church of Jesus Christ of Latter-day Saints excommunicated Professor Brodie. She considered the act a gift of liberation.

Mormons take comfort in the fact that groups of witnesses signed affidavits attesting to the existence of Smith's golden plates. These are remembered as The Three Witnesses and The Eight Witnesses. Their solemn oaths that the plates existed are included in every copy of the Book of Mormon. However, what these witnesses actually saw may not be what we imagine of witnesses today.

The translation of the Book of Mormon was completed in July 1829. There was an important step yet to complete.

The Book itself mentioned witnesses that should be allowed to see the golden plates. Smith knew the time had come. At a Sunday morning service in the Smith home, Joseph called Oliver Cowdery, David Whitmer, and Martin Harris to follow him into the woods. It was time for them to see the plates, he announced. They found a spot, humbled themselves, prayed, and waited. Nothing happened. They tried again. Nothing happened. Unable to take the strain, the ever uncertain Martin Harris jumped up and confessed that he must be the cause of their failure, that he was not as righteous as he should be. Removing himself to a distant spot, Harris prayed alone while the others continued. In a moment, an angel appeared. He was holding the golden plates. He turned each leaf one by one so all could see. Then, a voice: "These plates have been revealed by the power of God, and they have been translated by the power of God. The translation of them you have seen is correct, and I command you to bear record of what you now see and hear."

The angel left and Joseph ran to where Harris was praying. Then the two prayed together. Immediately, Harris experienced what the others had—the angel, the plates, the voice. "In an ecstasy of joy," Harris jumped to his feet and shouted, "'Tis enough; 'tis enough; mine eyes have beheld; mine eyes have beheld."[9]

There is another version of this experience that was offered later by Thomas Ford, the governor of Illinois. He knew some of the men who were witnesses to the plates, though he knew them years later when they were angry, separate from the

Church, and offended with the Prophet Joseph Smith. Ford recounted that the witnesses were "set to continual prayer, and other spiritual exercises." Finally, Smith assembled them in a room and produced a box which he said contained the plates. "The lid was open," Ford wrote, "the witnesses peeped into it, but making no discovery, for the box was empty, they said, 'Brother Joseph, we do not see the plates.' The prophet answered them, 'O ye of little faith! How long will God bear with this wicked and perverse generation? Down on your knees, brethren, every one of you, and pray God for the forgiveness of your sins, and for a holy and living faith which cometh down from heaven.'" The men did as they were told. This repenting lasted more than two hours. Finally, the men were allowed to peer again into the box: "they were now persuaded that they saw the plates."[10]

Like many moments in LDS history, this vague and questionable experience would come to mean much. The men with Smith would be known to history as "The Three Witnesses." Their testimony would affirm the truth of the angel Moroni, the golden plates, and the prophetic call of Joseph Smith for generations of Mormons. We should ponder this affirmation because it is among the two or three statements that puts certainty about Mormon beginnings in every Mormon heart.

> Be it known unto all nations, kindreds, tongues and people . . . that we, through the grace of God . . . have seen the plates which contain this record . . .

> And we also know that they have been translated by
> the gift and power of God . . . wherefore we know
> of a surety that the work is true. And we also testify
> that we have seen the engravings which are upon
> the plates; and they have been shown unto us by the
> power of God, and not of man. And we declare . . .
> that an angel of God came down from heaven . . . and
> he brought and laid before our eyes . . . the plates
> and the engravings thereon.[11]

Smith, knowing the importance of such testimony, wanted more men to be able to speak of the plates to the world. A few days after the angel appeared to the Three, Smith took eight men into the woods. These included Joseph Sr., his two sons (the prophet's brothers) Hyrum and Samuel, and the four sons of David Whitmer—Christian, Jacob, Peter Jr., and John—along with their brother-in-law, Hiram Page. After prayer and "secret devotions," Joseph showed the plates to his eight witnesses. Like the Three, the Eight issued a declaration of what they had seen.

> Be it known unto all nations, kindreds, tongues
> and people, unto whom this work shall come, that
> Joseph Smith, Jr. the Author and Proprietor of this
> work, has shewn unto us the plates which hath been
> spoken, which have the appearance of gold; and as
> many of the leaves as the said Smith has translated,

we did handle with our hands; and we also saw the engravings thereon, all of which has the appearance of ancient work, and of curious workmanship. And this we bear record, with words of soberness, that the said Smith has shewn unto us, for we have seen and hefted, and know of a surety that the said Smith has got the plates of which we have spoken. And we gave our names unto the world to witness unto the world that which we have seen: and we lie not, God bearing witness of it.[12]

It was signed by the three Smiths, the four Whitmers, and their brother-in-law. Mark Twain later quipped, "I could not feel more satisfied and at rest if the entire Whitmer family had testified."[13]

The eight men walked out of the woods exulting. They had seen the golden plates of God. Smith lingered behind. And then, not too surprisingly, the angel appeared. It was time, Smith later said, to yield up the plates. He surrendered them willingly, knowing that never again could another man expect to see them.

It is hard to escape the conclusion that Joseph Smith concocted revelations whenever he needed them. Even for those who believe prophecy and supernatural happenings are possible,

Smith's revelations seem to be self-serving, a product of his need and his will. The revelation that led to the Book of Mormon's printing is a prime example and we should note that it is symbolic of convenient revelations extending all throughout LDS history.

The story begins with Egbert Grandin, printer of the local *Wayne Sentinel*, agreeing to print Smith's book. The ever eager Martin Harris had guaranteed $3,000 for the printing of 5,000 copies and put his farm up for guarantee against further expenses. It was what his wife had feared but she was no longer an influence, Harris having put her out of his life with a settlement of eighty acres and a house.

All seemed on course until the citizens of Palmyra, most of them Christians, decided to boycott the publication of Joseph Smith's imaginings and the heresies it proclaimed. The printer Grandin became nervous, refused to print until he had the rest of his money, and this brought everything to a halt. Smith realized he had only one place to turn.

Martin Harris had a valuable farm and had pledged it against expenses to print this thrilling new book. The golden plates, the visitation of angels, the charisma of Joseph Smith—all inspired Harris and made him the anointed man he had always wanted to be. He had even prophesied. He warned Palmyra that it would be destroyed by 1836. He warned the nation that by 1838 Joseph Smith's new movement would make an American president unnecessary. He had even seen Jesus—

in the form of a deer, walking with him and talking with him as one man might another.

Smith saw that Harris was his source if the job was ever to get done. In an angry revelation to Smith, the Lord chastised Harris and even took note that Palmyra tongues were wagging about his relationship with the wife of another man. This could not continue.

> I command you to repent—repent, lest I smite you by the rod of my mouth, and by my wrath, and by mine anger, and your sufferings be sore.
>
> How sore you know not!
>
> How exquisite you know not!
>
> . . . And I command you that you preach nought but repentance and show not these things unto the world until it is wisdom in me. . . . And again, I command thee that thou shalt not covet thy neighbor's wife; nor seek thy neighbor's life. And again, I command thee that thou shalt not covet thine own property, but impart it freely to the printing of the Book of Mormon. . . .
>
> And misery thou shalt receive if thou wilt slight these counsels; yea, even the destruction of thyself and property. . . .
>
> Pay the printer's debt! Release thyself from bondage.[14]

A terrified Harris sold his farm and paid the printer. Grandin got busy printing and by March 26, 1830, the Book of Mormon was on sale in the lone Palmyra bookstore. The doctrines of the hat and the seer stone, of the golden plates and an angel named Moroni, of a 1,400-year-old civilization and the Christian apostles of centuries before—all were now unveiled to a watching, mystified world. It had only taken another Joseph Smith revelation to get it done.

CHAPTER 5

AN AMERICAN GOSPEL

I told the brethren that the Book of Mormon was the most correct of any book on earth, and the keystone of our religion, and a man would get nearer to God by abiding by its precepts, than by any other book.[1]

—Joseph Smith

"Dude, you've never even *read* the Book of Mormon?" The shirtless runner who asks this is Jason Garn. He and his buddy, Don Linder, are doing a "long run" before their interval training later in the afternoon. They're on the USC track team.

"No, I've never read it and I don't plan to."

"But all you *do* is bellyache about Mormons. I mean, your family goes to Hawaii, you come home griping about how the Mormons are taking over. We're watchin' the Final Four but all you can do is gripe about how nasty BYU set a comeback record. And you—you haven't even read their freakin' book?"

"No. Are you kidding? It's a nightmare to read. I'd rather be beat with a stick every day of my life."

"But then you have no credibility at all for the stuff you say, man. You've gotta read their book, for heaven's sake!"

"That's just not gonna happen. Listen, that thing is weird."

"I know, I know. My mother thinks the Book of Mormon was written by a demon."

"Yeah, a demon of boredom! Listen, all that voodoo stuff aside, the Book of Mormon is like the worst book ever. I mean I'm talking about just to read it, not anything else."

"Really?"

"Oh yes! Believe me, just the phrase *it came to pass* is probably used a million times. I only read a few pages before I passed out and I could have sworn the word *verily* was used twice that much on just one page. Most of the sentences begin with 'And.' I'm telling you, it's a snore!"

"Well, so it sounds just like the King James Bible then, huh?"

"Oh, much worse! And it's funny you say that because the real knock on the Book of Mormon is that it quotes the King James Bible so much."

"So what?"

"Well, it was supposedly compiled about 400 years after Jesus. So what's some dude livin' at that time doing quoting a version of the Bible that didn't exist until 1,200 years later?"

"How'd you learn all this stuff? You been watching PBS without me?"

"Dude, I read. I just don't read stuff coated in Ambien!"

"Still, man. You've got to read it if you're going to keep spouting off about the LDSers all the time."

"Look, I'm not saying anything everybody doesn't already know anyway. You remember Dr. Santiago talking about those Mormon missionaries that came to his house?"

"No. Why?"

"Doc asked them if they had read all the Book of Mormon."

"Yeah—and?"

"And they said no. Doc asked why they hadn't read it and they shrugged and said, 'We just couldn't get through it!'"

The two erupt with laughter until they realize they can either laugh or breathe.

"Oh, that's too rich!" Linder is still giggling as he says this. Jason expects more Mormon trivia but instead the two run a few miles in silence. He cuts his eyes to Linder and sees he's gone serious, that he's chewing on something in his head. There's nothing but the rhythm of their feet on the pavement and the wind.

Finally, Linder speaks, his voice low and even.

"You know, seriously, the thing that bugged me most about the Book of Mormon was that voice, and I—"

"What do you mean? I thought you only read a few pages."

"I read enough. And there's this voice. I mean if you get past all the 'yeas' and the 'verilys' and the 'and-it-came-to-passes,' there's this personality speaking that is bloated and haughty and—I don't know, maybe *domineering* is the word. It's irritating. Freaky."

"I thought it was written by a whole bunch of people, like the Bible."

"Yeah, that's my point. It's supposed to be. But there's this voice that you feel all the way through—I know, I know, but I jumped around when I read it!—and it starts to get gross how arrogant it is. I mean there are pages and pages where you haven't got a clue what's going on for all the high holy rambling but you're still runnin' up against that voice. I can't remember anything that book said but I'll always remember the feel of that voice."

The two run on in silence, drinking in the kind of peace only distance runners know. Then Jason looks over at Linder.

"What?" Linder says defensively.

"I'm just wondering how anything arrogant and bloated could bother *you*."

"That's it!"

Linder speaks no more. Instead, he starts to kick. He quickly, smoothly moves out in front. And Jason Garn knows he's about to get smoked.

When the Book of Mormon was first published on March 26, 1830, it sold for $1.25. Given the great heft of the work, it was a deal. Joseph Smith's mysterious tome reached to 275,000 words, stretched across almost 600 pages and invoked roughly 200 individually named characters. The story it told ranged over nearly a thousand years and recalled events from centuries before Christ. It truly was a *magnum opus*.

In the early days, both critics and believers called it variously the "Mormon Bible," the "Golden Bible," and, of course, "Joseph Smith's Bible." It was divided into fifteen "books," giving the structure a biblical feel, though, unlike the Bible, the Book of Mormon does not divide into sections of history, poetry, law, and prophecy. All its themes are interwoven. The fifteen books are usually named for the prophets featured in them. One name, Jacob, would have been familiar to the Christian world. Others were foreign: Helaman, Nephi, Mosiah, Omni, Moroni, and, certainly, Mormon. Nearly half the books were presented as unedited and directly from the pen of a prophet. The rest of the fifteen were compiled and edited by the prophet Mormon or his son, Moroni. This means that at times there are three narrative voices on the page.

The Book of Mormon claims to be a history of Jewish tribes in the New World. The saga unveiled in its pages begins with a Jewish prophet named Nephi who sailed to the New World around 600 BC, just before Babylonian invaders destroyed Jerusalem. Accompanied by his father, Lehi—who was also a prophet—Nephi settled in the western hemisphere with his five brothers, Laman, Lemuel, Sam, Jacob, and Joseph. By the time Lehi died, Nephi had won the loyalty of Jacob, Joseph, and Sam. This enraged older brothers, Laman and Lemuel, causing them to break from the family. The two branches of Lehi's clan went their separate ways. Nephi led his followers to a remote part of the continent while Laman and Lemuel remained where they were and grew ever more evil. In time, the rebellious "Lamanites" were cursed by the Lord, who "did cause a skin of blackness to come upon them." They were changed, God said, "that they might not be enticing unto my people"—meaning to the Nephites, who were "white and exceeding fair and delightful."

These two races grew powerful: the cursed, dark-skinned Lamanites and the blessed, light-skinned Nephites. There were wars, murders, and intrigues. Prophets spoke their prediction or their curses, battles ended with bodies heaped high, and always there were shallow graves left behind—an explanation for the burial mounds that bewitched the residents of New England.

Jesus Christ appeared to the Nephites during the days following his resurrection. He preached a message of love, forgiveness, and redemption that melted animosities and secured peace for more than 200 years. Satan did not rest during these centuries, though, and war eventually returned. In the shadow of a final, horrific battle, a prophet named Mormon carefully preserved the words of the prophets who had come before him. He translated the sacred writings into Reformed Egyptian—"as it had been handed down to him"—inscribed the words onto gold plates, and passed them to his son just before dying in the great Lamanite destruction of the Nephite world around AD 385. During the thirty-six years left of his life, Moroni wrote an additional twenty-four plates, known to history as the Book of Ether, which told the story of the Jaredites, a Semitic people who had sailed for the New World in 2500 BC "directly from the Tower of Babel." Moroni wrote a second book, one that bore his name, describing how ministry was done in the day of Christ. Finally, he buried the plates and died hoping for a day of restoration. Centuries later, that day came—on September 22, 1827, when Joseph Smith recovered the golden plates.

The Book of Mormon recounts an epic tale. If it is fruit of one man's imagination, then it is among the first uniquely American works of fiction. If it is from a supernatural source, then it is a kind of Western Scripture, a holy book unveiled to the citizens of the early American frontier.

It is usually ignored as serious literature outside of the Church. This is both because of its religious aura and also because it unfolds upon the emotional landscape of Joseph Smith. There is a prophet whose father is also a prophet and whose brothers are forced to decide whether they will acknowledge the anointed one among them. Special stones—not unlike Smith's beloved seer stones—provide light for the Jaredite ships that cross the sea to the New World. These stones have been touched by the finger of God, the same God who provides crystals to help the Jaredites navigate. This is clearly Smith's imprint upon the page—if, indeed, the entire work is not Smith's imprint upon the page. Prophets are astonishingly holy and seers are seldom wrong and, as one historian has noted, "in three thousand years not a single harlot was made to speak."[2] All of this has caused scholars to back away and has left the Book of Mormon in an academic "no man's land," tended lovingly only by the LDS faithful.

There are moments of beauty in the text. In the Book of Jacob, for example, a figure laments, "Our lives passed away, like as it were unto us a dream, we being a lonesome and a solemn people, wanderers, cast out from Jerusalem."[3] Yet there is no question that the book is its own worst enemy. Its stylistic oddities, factual inaccuracies, often mind-numbing narrative, and near allegorical treatment of early nineteenth-century themes work against its claim to be Scripture and against its appeal as literature. These features of the text have defined battle lines that faithful Mormons have been forced to defend since the days of Joseph Smith.

Early readers of the Book of Mormon could be forgiven for thinking they had stumbled onto some unfamiliar portion of their family Bible. More than 27,000 words in Smith's writing came straight from that Bible, nearly 10 percent of the whole. The style was unmistakable. The phrase "and it came to pass" is used more than 2,000 times and others, like "verily I say unto you," "and whosoever," or "for behold," make the book sound like the King James Bible's little brother. This should come as no surprise. The Book of Mormon's plundering of the Bible is flagrant. Poor Isaiah took particular abuse. One character alone quotes thirteen consecutive chapters of Isaiah and this is part of a broader free-for-all in which twenty-one chapters of Isaiah are quoted in part or in full. Other biblical books come in for similar treatment.

Entire Bible stories appear, sometimes lightly adapted for New World use. A woman dances before a king and it leads to a decapitation—as in the biblical story of Salome. A character named Aminadi deciphers handwriting on a wall and another named Alma is converted in exactly the same way as the apostle Paul. Ammon—apparently not finding a Goliath—slays instead sheep rustlers of a kind familiar to Joseph Smith's readers.

Mark Twain was so induced to slumber by the thousands of *yea*s, *and*s, and *behold*s that he called the Book of Mormon "chloroform in print."[4] Joseph Smith's scribes had not been educated enough to understand the rules of punctuation and this left printers to divide sentences wherever they thought best. It meant, for example, that of the first 200 sentences in the book, 140 began with "And."[5]

There are mistakes too—or perhaps they are corrections. Jesus is born in Jerusalem. John baptizes in the village of "Bethabara." Horses are brought to the New World thousands of years before Columbus' time—though there were none here when the admiral arrived in 1492. Nor were there pigs or sheep or cattle or donkeys—all of which the Jaredites brought in with them in 2500 BC, according to the Book of Mormon.

There is some recognition in the text of the Book of Mormon itself that errors might have been made. Even the man/angel Moroni makes excuses: "And if our plates had been sufficiently large we should have written in Hebrew; but the Hebrew hath been altered by us also, and if we could have written in Hebrew ye would have had none imperfection in our record." The title page also appears to warn of something amiss: "Now if there be fault, it be the mistake of men." These same words, repeated at the end of the book, are followed by, "But behold, we know no fault. Nevertheless, God knoweth all things; therefore he that condemneth, let him be aware lest he shall be in danger of hell fire."

The most searing indictment of the Book of Mormon is the way the story it tells seems to grow organically from the soil of the United States in the early 1800s. Settlers from the east come west by ship to escape an evil system. They settle in a New World and must battle for survival against a darker-skinned enemy. One expects the *Mayflower* and Squanto to be mentioned by name. There is a secret society called the Gadiantons who sound uncannily like the Freemasons of Joseph Smith's time. There are also thinly veiled bombasts against the Roman Catholic Church. The Nephites conduct democratic elections; the New World is referred to as "the land of liberty." It is an allegory of America.

Or maybe New York. Alexander Campbell, a father of the American restoration movement, famously captured this historical dislocation when he wrote, "This prophet Smith, through his stone spectacles, wrote on the plates of Nephi, in his Book of Mormon, every error and almost every truth discussed in New York for the last ten years. He decided all the great controversies:—infant baptism, ordination, the trinity, regeneration, repentance, justification, the fall of man, the atonement, transubstantiation, fasting, penance, church government, religious experience, the call to the ministry, the general resurrection, eternal punishment, who may baptize and even the question of free masonry, republican government and the right of man. . . . But he is better skilled in the controversies in New York than in the geography or history of Judea."[6] As dissident LDS historian Fawn Brodie has concluded, "if his [Smith's] book is monotonous today, it is because the frontier fires are long since dead and the burning questions that the book answered are ashes."[7]

Even the unlikely choice of "Reformed Egyptian" for the Book of Mormon's original language shows an element of chronological misalignment. While Smith stared at seer stones in his hat, it was widely believed that Egyptian hieroglyphics could not be deciphered, that the intriguing ancient symbols would forever be a dead language for modern men. The Prophet had likely seen a June 1, 1827, article in his local paper in which hieroglyphics from Mexico were offered as proof that Mexicans and Egyptians "had intercourse with each other, and . . . had the same system of mythology."[8] This was inaccurate, but it may have planted a seed.

Smith could not have known that the "code" of the Rosetta Stone, discovered in Egypt in 1799 and deciphered by French scholar Jean Francoise Champollion in 1822, would allow Egyptologists to interpret hieroglyphics with increasing accuracy over the next decades. This led to many an embarrassing moment for Smith's lieutenants, who naively tried to secure scholarly confirmation of Smith's translation work. It never came.

The truth is that the underlying thesis of the Book of Mormon was nothing new to those living when Smith was claiming revelation. The idea that the American Indians were descendants of the "Lost Tribes" of Israel was common. Nearly every well-known minister believed it, from Cotton Mather to William Penn. Jonathan Edwards, perhaps the greatest theologian of the American colonial era, had written about it in the mid-1700s. Indeed, it was not an idea unknown to Columbus.

So accepted was this theory that it was treated in a leading book, a book that some scholars believe was used by Joseph Smith to craft his revelations. It was called *View of the Hebrews, or the Ten Tribes of Israel in America.*[9] It was written by a Vermont pastor named Ethan Smith and was published in 1823. A second edition came two years later. Even if Joseph Smith never read this book, *View of the Hebrews* confirms that the general worldview of the Book of Mormon—and many of its details—were available apart from revelation. The similarities between the two books are stunning.

Ethan Smith believed of the Indians what the Book of Mormon assumed: "Israel brought into this new continent a considerable degree of civilization; and the better part of them long laboured to maintain it. But others fell into the hunting and consequently savage state; whose barbarous hordes invaded their more civilized brethren, and eventually annihilated most of them, and all in these northern regions."[10] It is easy to see in these words a rationale for tribes something like the Lamanites and the Nephites, a believable explanation for their distinct natures, and an explanation for the ultimate destruction of the one by the other.

Smith also suggested the idea of a lost book of revelation. An ancient Hebrew phylactery had been unearthed in Massachusetts. This stirred excitement in the area, as did the legend of a chief who claimed that his people "had long since a book which they had for a long time preserved. But having lost the knowledge of reading it, they concluded it would be of no further use to them; and they buried it with an Indian chief."[11] This legend was well known at the time. The sensationalist historian and novelist Josiah Priest recounted it in his *American Antiquities*, and Joseph Smith in turn quoted Priest in an article he wrote for his church newspaper in 1833.

Fawn Brodie has helpfully summarized much of the common ground between the Book of Mormon and *View of the Hebrews*:

Both books opened with frequent references to the destruction of Jerusalem; both told of inspired prophets among the ancient Americans; both quoted copiously and almost exclusively from Isaiah; and both delineated the ancient Americans as a highly civilized people. Both held that it was the mission of the American nation in the last days to gather these remnants of the house of Israel and bring them to Christianity, thereby hastening the day of the glorious millennium.[12]

Ethan Smith even mentioned that copper breastplates recovered from Indian mounds were "in resemblance of the Urim and Thummim." He suggested that the Mexican god Quetzalcoatl was a "Christ figure." He mentioned the crosses that were occasionally discovered in native mounds as confirmation that the gospel of Jesus Christ, if not Christ himself, had come to the New World long before white settlers.

There was much more and all of it might have suggested to a fertile imagination like Joseph Smith's the entire scheme of the Book of Mormon. The Prophet not only knew of the Vermont pastor's popular study of Hebrews in America but he was also familiar with its contents. Assume that Smith did not receive the Book of Mormon by revelation as he claimed and it is not going too much further to believe that he must have used sources just like Ethan Smith's *View of the Hebrews*.

Yet Ethan Smith's *View of the Hebrews* was not the only book the Mormon Prophet might have used—if, that is, he was not genuinely guided by some supernatural force. Novels also toyed with the theory that the American Indians were lost Jewish tribes and one in particular—*Manuscript Found* by Solomon Spaulding—was so much like the Book of Mormon that it heaps even greater suspicion on Joseph Smith than *View of the Hebrews*.

Spaulding's *Manuscript Found* has long defined battle lines among students of Mormon history. It so parallels Joseph Smith's revelations that some scholars have insisted it must have been at least one of Smith's sources. There is also a complicated conspiracy theory in which Sidney Rigdon, a Mormon convert and Joseph Smith confidant, reworked the original Spaulding novel to create what became the Book of Mormon. LDS scholars, of course, reject this out of hand. The debate will never end. It involves an inviting *DaVinci Code*–like literary mystery, it is rooted in deep-seated religious passion, and there are scholarly egos on the line.

The story begins with an offended ex-Mormon named Philastus Hurlbut who heard of Spaulding's novel in 1833. By then, Spaulding was dead but Hurlbut determined to interview anyone who could testify to the content of *Manuscript Found*, since no copy had survived. If half of what Hurlbut's witnesses recounted was true, it is hard not to conclude that Joseph Smith plagiarized. Spaulding's brother John, for example, reported that the novel described "the first settlers of America, endeavoring to show that the American Indians are the descendants of the Jews, or the lost tribes." The author gave "a detailed account of their journey from Jerusalem, by land and sea, till they arrived in America, under the command of Nephi and Lehi." The family of these men fought and separated into "Nephites" and "Lamanites." There was a great war between the two in which multitudes were slain and the dead were buried "in great heaps, which caused the mounds so common in this country." The author's brother concluded, "I have recently read the Book of Mormon, and to my great surprise I find nearly the same historical matter, names, etc., as they were in my brother's writings."

Solomon Spaulding's sister-in-law, Martha, remembered *Manuscript Found* being read to her and distinctly recalled "the names of Nephi, and Lehi" as "officers of the company which first came off from Jerusalem." Hurlbut also interviewed six of Spaulding's neighbors, each of whom gave similar testimony. One said he had read the Book of Mormon and "was astonished to find the same passages in it that Spaulding had read to me more than twenty years before." Another said that "many of the passages in the Mormon book are verbatim from Spaulding," and cited the names Nephi, Lehi, Moroni, "and in fact all the principal names" as originating in *Manuscript Found*. Yet another remembered the often-repeated phrase "I, Nephi" and recalled that Spaulding had hoped that "after this generation had passed away, his account of the first inhabitants of America would be considered as authentic as any other history."[13]

What these testimonies reveal is that the outline of history assumed in the Book of Mormon could have come from sources other than revelation. Joseph Smith was not launching into new territory but was rather imagining—or having revealed to him—an extension of what might easily have been learned from popular books, from newspaper articles, from conversations with well-read townsfolk, and even from excited conversation in the village tavern. If Smith was not spiritually directed in writing the founding text of Mormonism, it would have been little challenge for a mind such as his to weave a rich religious tapestry from the raw historical material he undoubtedly already knew.

This brings us to an all-important question: is the Book of Mormon based in fact? Did the cities it mentions exist? Is there evidence for the people it describes? Is its geography similar to anything scholars can confirm? Are there other records or inscriptions written in a language approaching "Reformed Egyptian"?

Some prefer to lay these questions aside. Martin Marty, legendary University of Chicago historian, wants to "seek to understand" Joseph Smith's message rather than try to assess its accuracy. One of the leading scholars of Mormonism, Jan

Shipps—who is not a Mormon herself—hopes to understand how the Mormons' "sacred myth" shapes lives and history, but she is less interested in questions of historical fact. This is in keeping with the majority of religious scholars, who often ask, "Who cares what a religion says about happenings centuries ago? What does it mean to us now?"

This might work for more ethereal religions that hover over time and space without laying claim to either. The religion of Joseph Smith is not one of them. Mormons declare themselves on a vast array of historical matters which they regard as the fruit of revelation. They insist that Jews settled in the New World around the time of the ancient Tower of Babel. Still other Jews did the same at about the time Babylon conquered Jerusalem. Jackson County, Missouri, was the site of the Garden of Eden. There was a language called "Reformed Egyptian" spoken and written in the New World as late as AD 400. Native Americans today are the descendants of ancient Jews. All of this and more has been revealed.

A historical faith that makes historical assertions demands to be measured on the basis of historical accuracy. Mormon leaders themselves have understood this and, to their credit, have said so publicly. LDS president Gordon Hinckley said in a PBS interview in 2007, "It's either true or false. If it's false, we're engaged in a great fraud. If it's true, it's the most important thing in the world." A professor at Brigham Young University, Louis Midgley, argued, "To reduce the Book of Mormon to mere myth weakens, if not destroys, the possibility of it witnessing to the truth about divine things. A fictional Book of Mormon fabricated by Joseph Smith, even when his inventiveness, genius, or 'inspiration' is celebrated, does not witness to Jesus Christ but to human folly. A true Book of Mormon is a powerful witness; a fictional one is hardly worth reading and pondering."[14]

It is an admirable stand, but if it is the stand of the Church of the Latter-day Saints in the modern world, the Church has much work to do. In fact, it may be in deep trouble. The truth is that when all of the research is considered, there is precious little scientific or historical evidence that Book of Mormon claims are historically true. Spiritually? Perhaps. Historically? Not likely. There is, for example, no unimpeachable evidence that the language Smith called "Reformed Egyptian" ever existed. The geography of the Book of Mormon is almost entirely unconfirmed. Nor is there evidence that the DNA of Native Americans is remotely related to the DNA of Hebrews or any other significant Semitic people.

It would seem too that final verdicts on these matters have been rendered again and again. As long ago as 1973, Michael Coe, former professor of anthropology at Yale, gave the devastating verdict from which most scholars have not departed. In a *Dialogue* article, Coe wrote, "The bare facts of the matter are that nothing, absolutely nothing, has ever shown up in any New World excavation which would suggest to a dispassionate observer that the Book of Mormon, as claimed by Joseph Smith, is a historical document relating to the history of early migrants to our hemisphere." It got worse. After using terms like "ridiculous" and "myth" to describe LDS claims, Coe concluded, "To me, as a sympathetic and interested outsider . . . the efforts . . . to go beyond the moral and ethical content of the Book of Mormon arouse feelings not of superiority but of compassion: the same kind of compassion that one feels for persons who are engaged on quests that have been, are now, and always will be unproductive."

Mormon scholars have come to some of the same conclusions. One of the most intriguing examples is that of B. H. Roberts. Asked by an LDS president in the 1920s to develop apologetic approaches for common Book of Mormon problems, Roberts eventually turned to Ethan Smith's *View of the Hebrews*. He wrote an analysis of the parallels between the two books but then died before it was published. His study did not come to light for almost fifty years when it was published by the University of Illinois Press in 1985. Though a devoted Mormon, Roberts wrote:

> In the light of this evidence, there can be no doubt as to the possession of a vividly strong, creative imagination by Joseph Smith, the Prophet, an imagination, it could with reason be urged, which, given the suggestions that are to be found in the "common knowledge" of accepted American antiquities of the times, supplemented by such a work as Ethan Smith's

View of the Hebrews, would make it possible for him to create a book such as the Book of Mormon is.[15]

In other words, Joseph Smith had probably not received revelation. He had imagined the Book of Mormon using the raw material of knowledge common in his day, Ethan Smith's work in particular. Only the fact that Roberts was dead kept him from being excommunicated like other LDS scholars who had drawn the same conclusion. It helped too that he had been an LDS General Authority.

If all this is true, then why has there been no mass exodus from the LDS Church? In part, it is because Mormon scholars still valiantly hope for factual confirmation of their faith. The work of organizations like FARMS, the Foundation for Ancient Research and Mormon Studies—now associated with the Neal Maxwell Institute for Religious Scholarship at BYU—is the product of this vision.

Yet most Latter-day Saints are not primarily interested in scholarship. They are taught to seek a testimony, a confirmation of the Spirit, as to the truth of their faith. From their earliest days, their leaders urge them to ask God "if these things are not true; and if ye shall ask with a sincere heart, with real intent, having faith in Christ, he will manifest the truth of it unto you, by the power of the Holy Ghost" (Moroni 10:4). In other words, the matter of ultimate truth is not a matter of science; it is a matter of having an "inner knowing" given by the Holy Spirit.

This approach can tend to make scholarship unimportant. As Joseph Fielding Smith, the nephew of the Prophet and an LDS president, once wrote: "It is the personal opinion of the writer that the Lord does not intend that the Book of Mormon, at least at the present time, shall be proved true by any archaeological findings. The day may come when such will be the case, but not now. The Book of Mormon is itself a witness of the truth, and the promise has been given most solemnly that any person who will read it with a prayerful heart may receive the aiding testimony of its truth."

It is a pious sentiment but it will seem to most outsiders like an excuse: Mormons make dramatic statements about history but then claim God does not intend for the facts that support those statements to be proven. It is frustrating, intellectually unsatisfying, and perhaps even duplicitous, but it is consistent with what every Mormon repeatedly affirms—"I have received the witness of the Spirit, and I bear testimony that the Book of Mormon is true."

Mormon Beliefs in Plain Language

1. Not long after the Christian Church began, the pure teachings of Jesus Christ were lost or perverted. By the early 1800s, all Christian churches had become corrupt, had distorted the true gospel of Jesus Christ, and were an "abomination" to God.

2. Beginning in 1820, the Prophet Joseph Smith experienced a series of spiritual visitations in which the Aaronic and Melchizedek priesthoods were "restored" and through which the Book of Mormon was recovered and translated.

3. The Book of Mormon teaches that tribes of Jews settled in the New World first at the time of the Tower of Babel and then again at the time of the Babylonian destruction of Jerusalem, around 600 BC. Jesus Christ visited the descendants of these tribes after his resurrection. His teachings as well as the history of these warring Jewish tribes were recorded on gold plates and buried around AD 400. Guided by the angel Moroni, Joseph Smith recovered these plates and translated them, thus producing the Book of Mormon in the early 1800s.

4. The Church of Jesus Christ of Latter Day Saints (LDS) was formed on April 6, 1830, with Joseph Smith as its First Elder. Mormons consider it "the only living and true Church" on earth. Today, it is led by a President who is regarded as "prophet, seer, and revelator." He is aided by Twelve Apostles. There is also a Quorum of the Seventy who help govern the church. These together are called The General Authorities.

5. All men have existed as spirits before assuming physical bodies on earth. During this "premortality," families were already formed and destinies determined. The noble spirits in this preexistence become Mormons when they live on earth. The ignoble spirits of preexistence are non-Mormons on earth.

6. The God of this planet, usually referred to as "Heavenly Father," was once a man. He now leads a family that rules earth with him. They are spiritual beings but since they are a purer form of spirit, they have an elevated type of physical body. Jesus and Lucifer are brothers, both sons of Heavenly Father. There is also a Heavenly Mother.

7. When Heavenly Father was devising a plan for populating the earth, Jesus and Lucifer both offered proposals. Jesus' plan was chosen and Lucifer's was rejected. Lucifer rebelled and a third of the premortal spirits followed him. There was a great war in the heavens. Jesus was then sent to earth as a loving savior. Mary became pregnant with Jesus as a result of Heavenly Father having physical intercourse with her.

8. Adam and Eve were actually gods who made a heroic choice in eating the forbidden fruit. Their choice made mortal life possible which then gave all preexistent spirits an opportunity to live on earth and qualify for celestial glory.

9. Life on earth is best understood as a time of testing in order to qualify for eternal exaltation.

10. The death of Jesus Christ introduces men to Heavenly Father but then men must obey the laws and ordinances of the gospel themselves in order to be saved.

11. In the same way that Heavenly Father was once a man, faithful members of the Church may one day become gods. This is called The Law of Eternal Progression and has been summarized in LDS history in these words: "As man is, God was; as God is, man may become." Most Mormons expect to rule planets with their families once they achieve ultimate salvation.

12. The Book of Mormon is the word of Heavenly Father. The Bible is also the word of Heavenly Father, but only after it is correctly translated. Mormons believe that the original Bible was corrupted through the centuries and that the Bible as it exists today is missing many "plain and precious parts." Joseph Smith made a new version of the Bible by revising more than 3,400 verses on the basis of new revelation he had received. Some Mormons use Smith's version of the Bible today, but the main LDS body uses the King James Version since Smith's version was never finished.

13. Joseph Smith was visited first by John the Baptist and then by Peter, James, and John, among others. In these visitations, the authority of the true priesthood of God was imparted. Men, but never women, usually assume this priesthood at the age of fourteen if they qualify. Priesthood authority empowers men to receive revelations and to act in God's name.

14. The Temple is a sacred place in which holy ceremonies, such as weddings, sealings, and endowments, are conducted. Gentiles, or non-Mormons, are not permitted in any of the LDS Temples around the world after the Temple is consecrated. Temple ceremonies are kept secret to preserve their sacredness.

15. One of the Temple ceremonies grants the LDS faithful a "Temple garment." This is never to be removed except for bathing and intercourse. When it wears out, it is to be burned. This garment reminds the Church member of vows to God and provides spiritual protection.

16. Before 1978, the Church regarded dark skin as the sign of a spiritual curse and so denied the priesthood to black men. Since 1978, black males may enter the priesthood.

17. Prior to the age of eight, the "age of accountability," children are without sin and do not need to be baptized. If they die before reaching this age, they enter directly into celestial exaltation. After this age, they are accountable for their sins and must be baptized and undergo all that is required for adults to achieve salvation.

18. Church members are required to tithe 10 percent of their incomes, to abstain from alcohol, tobacco, and caffeine, to attend meetings of their stakes and wards, to undergo Temple rituals, to submit to Church authorities, to fast once a month and give the money to the poor, and to hold a Family Home Evening on Monday nights—a time of teaching, discussion, and games.

19. Young men between the ages of nineteen and twenty-one are expected to serve on a mission for two years. The Church trains these missionaries and then assigns them to a post somewhere in the world. These men remain at their posts and do not return home during the entire two years. They are allowed to call home only twice, at Christmas and at Mother's Day. Women are now allowed to go on missions as well, though the Church continues to teach that missions are primarily for men.

20. Joseph Smith practiced polygamy or "plural marriage" and taught that it was essential to celestial exaltation. In 1890, President Wilford Woodruff officially forbade the practice, though it has been continued by some Latter-day Saints until today.

21. The United States of America is divinely ordained. The Garden of Eden was originally where the state of Missouri is now. Jesus will return to Jackson County, Missouri, when he returns. The US Constitution was divinely inspired.

22. Church members may be baptized for the dead. This allows those who have departed the opportunity to embrace the truth in eternity and then to begin their eternal progression toward exaltation.

23. Church members may also be "sealed" to their spouse and their children "for all eternity." These sealings are exclusively Temple ceremonies. There are other Temple ceremonies in which members are "endowed" with spiritual powers and receive revelations critical to their ultimate salvation.

24. God is continuing to reveal truth. This is called "progressive revelation." A president of the Church today may be given new revelation that overrides earlier revelation. An LDS president expressed this belief as the confidence that "a living prophet trumps a dead prophet." There may also be scriptures yet to be discovered.

25. Miracles, signs and wonders, healings, speaking in tongues, prophecy, and visions are possible for the faithful today.

26. Education in spiritual and temporal matters is vital since the knowledge gained in life on earth will be retained throughout all eternity.

27. At the return of Jesus Christ to earth, the millennium will begin and the world will be ruled from a Temple in Jerusalem and a Temple in Jackson County, Missouri.

CHAPTER 6

A NEW BREED OF MEN

This Priesthood . . . holds the keys of revelation of the oracles of God to man upon the earth; the power and right to give laws and commandments to individuals, churches, rulers, nations and the world; to appoint, ordain, and establish constitutions and kingdoms, to appoint kings, presidents, governors or judges.[1]

—Parley P. Pratt, LDS Apostle

"Honey, what's that box on the coffee table?"

"It's a gift for Oliver's son, Daniel. By the way, I'm on call for him tomorrow night. He's hosting some big celebration for his boy."

"No problem. I'm thinkin' sushi, wine, Jacuzzi, and movie right here at home for me. It's been a long week. What's the big occasion for Danny?"

"Their church is making him a priest, I think."

"A pr——a priest? Of what? I mean, the kid's twelve!"

"I know, but that's when they do it. As early as twelve. It's a big thing to them."

"What a crock! A priest at twelve years old?! What could he possibly know at that age?"

"Well, I asked Oliver and he said it's not primarily about knowledge. It's about spiritual power. So they do it young."

"Listen, I love Oliver and Jan, but their religion is a joke. Between the underwear and the no drinking and Proposition 8 and now their priests that are all of twelve. It's hard to take seriously."

"Yeah, I get it, but listen to this. Oliver told me a story about how big this priesthood thing is for them. You remember that book you loved on Jefferson?"

"*Thomas Jefferson: An Intimate Biography* by Fawn Brodie? Loved it! I mean, *loved it*. One of my all-time favorites."

"Well, I guess you know she also wrote a book on Joseph Smith."

"Sure. Read it too. What a great read and what a total liar he was. You wouldn't bel—"

"Hold up! Hold up! What I'm saying is that here she is, this huge historian from UCLA, and she writes all these big biographies. And the one on Smith gets her booted from the Mormon Church, right? She doesn't seem to care. Doesn't even try to appeal it."

"Good for her. Their version of their history is like something out of Disney anyway."

"All right. Well, so the book on Smith comes out in, what, 19 . . . ?"

"1945. Last year of World War II. I know the whole story."

"Well, you probably don't know this. It's 1980, she's dying of cancer. Metastatic lung, I think. Okay, it's been thirty-five years since she got kicked out of the Church. But her brother comes to visit her in the hospital. They've been estranged. And while he's visiting, she asks for what they call a 'priesthood blessing.' Can you believe it? She's one of the biggest critics of Smith and the Church, but she asks her priest brother for some kind of Mormon blessing."

"You're kidding!"

"No. And a few days later, she writes a note saying no one should think she wants anything to do with the Church just because she asked for the blessing. It's the last thing she ever wrote. Unbelievable, isn't it?"

"Amazing. I guess that stuff never leaves you once you take it in."

"I thought Oliver was exaggerating a bit but he's got a biography of her in his office and this story is right there on the page."

"I'm stunned. I wonder what she was thinking. She was such a strong woman and then, you know, there she is at the end caving in."

"I don't know. But I'll tell you what. If this priesthood blessing stuff works, I'm going to get young Daniel down at the office and get him blessing these ladies and then I can have some time off!"

"Get out of here!"

"Off to rounds. Love you."

The Church of Jesus Christ of Latter-day Saints is the success it is today in part because of characteristics that were present on the day of its birth. To understand these, we must first know a bit more about the occasion of that birth.

It was April 6, 1830, less than two weeks after the Book of Mormon reached the public on March 26. The time had come, though. Joseph Smith had been given a revelation. It was time for the "Church of Christ" to be "organized."

When some thirty of the faithful gathered at David Whitmer's farmhouse on that Tuesday, six men took the lead—Joseph, his brother Hyrum, their brother Samuel, Oliver Cowdery, and Peter and David Whitmer. The little congregation was asked if they would receive these six as fit to teach the truths of the Kingdom of God. All said they would. Joseph laid his hands upon Cowdery and ordained him an Elder. Cowdery in turn ordained Smith. It was what John the Baptist had proclaimed to the two nearly a year before. All took bread and wine to sanctify the moment and then Smith and Cowdery laid hands on each one there. Smith wrote later that the Holy Ghost descended. This was standard language from the revivals of previous years. It meant that some present began to react to the Spirit's work. A few began prophesying. Others loudly rejoiced.

Instantly, Smith received a revelation. He should ordain others as the Spirit led. Remembering the offices in the Book of Mormon's Nephite churches, he began ordaining elders, priests, and teachers. He was also told that "there shall be a record kept among you" and that in this record he would be "called a seer, a translator, a prophet, an apostle of Jesus Christ, an elder of the church through the will of God the Father, and the grace of your Lord Jesus Christ."

The priesthood. It is the heart of the Mormon religion. It had been restored, the Saints believe, while Smith was translating his plates. On May 15, 1829, he and Oliver Cowdery took a break from their work and walked into the woods. They would say later they had been convicted by something from the unfinished Book. While the two repented of their sins, Cowdery had a vision. As he recounted later, in the airy phrases of early Mormonism, "The voice of the Redeemer spake peace to us, while the veil was parted and the angel of God came down clothed with glory, and delivered the anxiously looked for message, and the keys of the Gospel of repentance . . . as we heard we rejoiced, while his love enkindled our souls, and we were rapt in the vision of the Almighty! Where was room for doubt? Nowhere; uncertainty had fled, doubt had sunk, no more to rise, while fiction and deception had fled forever."[2]

Afterward, Joseph declared that the angel was actually John the Baptist, who conferred upon the two men the true Hebraic priesthood of Aaron and ordered them to baptize each other. Over time, this remembrance evolved into Smith's more full-bodied version in *Pearl of Great Price*.

> A messenger from heaven descended in a cloud of light, having laid his hands upon us, he ordained us, saying: *Upon you my fellow servants, in the name of Messiah, I confer the priesthood of Aaron, which holds the keys of the ministering of angels, and of the gospel of repentance, and of baptism by immersion for the remission of sins; and this shall never be taken again from the earth until the sons of Levi do offer again an offering unto the Lord in righteousness.*
>
> He said this Aaronic priesthood had not the power of laying on hands for the gifts of the Holy Ghost, but that this should be conferred upon us hereafter; and he commanded us to go and be baptized. . . . The messenger who visited us on this occasion and conferred this priesthood upon us, said that his name was John, the same that is called John the Baptist in the New Testament, and that he acted under the direction of Peter, James and John, who held the keys of the priesthood of Melchizedek, which priesthood, he said, would in due time be conferred on us, and that I should be called the first Elder of the Church, and he (Oliver Cowdery) the second.

Smith and Cowdery reported that just days later they were visited by the apostles Peter, James, and John. These glorified beings held "the keys of the kingdom and of the Dispensation of the Fullness of Times." The three apostles ordained the two mortals to the "Melchizedek Priesthood," which empowered them to bestow the gifts of the Holy Ghost. Mormons hold that this occurred between May 15 and 29, 1829, and between Colesville, New York, and Harmony, Pennsylvania.

The astonishing claim that John the Baptist and the apostles Peter, James, and John visited two men in a New York woods in the 1820s tends to distract from the more important matter— to Mormons, anyway—of a bedrock truth of Mormonism: the Church of Jesus Christ of Latter-day Saints is the restoration of the priesthood of God. This was new. Traditional Christians had long believed that all the priesthoods of their Old Testament found their end in Jesus Christ, their high priest of all ages since his resurrection from the dead. Mormons maintain, instead, that *they* are the restoration of both the Aaronic priesthood—another name for the priesthood under the Mosaic law—and the Melchizedek priesthood, named for that unique, mystical Old Testament figure who was so great even the patriarch Abraham bowed to him.

This priesthood is the key to understanding all that Mormonism claims. Since their men can be priests, it means there is prophecy, healing, divine revelation, authority to rule and declare, and certainly power for contending with darkness. It means that written revelations yield their true meaning, that new revelations may be greater in authority to revelations of old, and that visitations of heavenly beings—like those known by Cowdery and Smith—ought to be nothing strange. In short, the restoration of the priesthood meant to Mormons the restoration of everything the corrupt Christian church had lost or perverted. Finally, the restored Gospel is available to men.

The beginning of the LDS Church includes nearly every feature of Mormonism that has made the religion a modern success. First, from the beginning there was the emphasis upon organizing. It is hard to exaggerate. The kind of administrative structure that most religions hope to evolve over time was there on the Saints' first day. For a movement led by lightly educated farmers and craftsmen, the Mormons showed an astonishing organizational gift. In their very first months they organized missionary outreaches, benevolent societies, sales efforts, and a sophisticated ecclesiastical structure. In time they organized entire cities, soaring Temples, and even vast stretches of the American West. It seemed to be the will of God. Between 1831 and 1837, sixty-five of Joseph Smith's revelations had to do with some administrative matter in the Church.[3]

A second vital feature of the Saints from their very first day was their total devotion to the supernatural. This comes as some surprise to those who see today's tightly orchestrated, clean-cut, almost manically disciplined Saints, storm troopers of the Heavenly Father, and find it hard to picture them as over-heated Pentecostals. The truth is that what the modern world has come to associate with Oral Roberts and Benny Hinn, with T. D. Jakes and the African American church experience, was standard fare among the Latter Day Saints.

It is impossible to understand Mormonism through the years without having some sense of this aspect of its culture. The Saints lived in constant expectation of supernatural events. They spoke in tongues, prayed for healing, thought nothing of someone being overcome by the Holy Spirit in their meetings, and treated prophecy as a way of life. To be among the Saints was to be near the edge of eternity, a place where revelations came, angels appeared, and a man might leave his farm and move his family across country based on a single dream. In a culture such as this, the particularly anointed rose fast. Men were known for having certain gifts, such as prophesying about the gender of unborn children or discerning if demons were tormenting an ailing calf. One man in particular was known for speaking in tongues and in an impressive and commanding fashion. It brought him to the attention of Joseph Smith and caused the Saints to trust him and quickly grant him a position of authority among them. His name was Brigham Young.

Early Mormons relied on the intervention of the invisible not just for vast revelations of doctrine and happenings in other worlds but for daily decisions. They were willing to suspend their own reasoning for direction they thought was from God. It was nothing for Joseph Smith or some other Elder or Priest to have a vision about how a man ought to tend his farm or what town a missionary ought to visit. Men rebuked each other not for what they had actually done but for what the Spirit had whispered in the night. Any belief could be overturned, any reputation acquired through character over years could be brought into question, and any seemingly sensible course could be redirected if a revelation came. What men heard from the Spirit was more certain to them than anything printed on a page or believed for generations. It was this sense of being on the very front edge of what the Holy Spirit was saying to their age that made Mormons willing to follow their Prophet no matter the pain, or to revise how they had thought for decades if a "word from God" required. This was the fire that kept the Mormon steel malleable—particularly in the hands of Joseph Smith.

Another Mormon ingenuity evident from the first day was how it seemed to offer a democratized religion while maintaining the Prophet's control. On the same day Joseph Smith proclaimed himself seer, translator, prophet, apostle, and elder, he began handing out titles and roles freely. This fit the age. The LDS Church was born in a country that had proclaimed itself a *novus ordo seculorum*—a "new order of the ages." The Saints lived in a new day, in a new country, in reach of a new and untrammeled frontier and they saw themselves, like most Americans, as a new breed of men. It was the age of Andrew Jackson and "every man a king" and of *Vox populi, vox Dei*—the "voice of the people is the voice of God." The new American would not sit still for spiritual experiences mediated by clergymen. They wanted an instantaneous experience and they wanted it on their own authority. This is what Joseph Smith offered. Every male Mormon was a priest, an elder, a deacon, a patriarch, an apostle, or a prophet of some kind and felt himself individually honored and empowered. All the while, Smith led the Saints as a benevolent dictator, his word nearly the word of God. This tension was part of the ingenious Mormon system.

Finally, there was the command that "there shall be a record kept among you." These words have made the Latter-day Saints among the most fastidious historians of any religious group in history. To document their journey was not simply a matter of eagerness to see their story told. It was a commandment. It was divinely ordained that precise records should be kept. This protected them from relying on outsiders to preserve their heritage. They could pass on to their children and grandchildren a version of their history shaped by the distinctives of their faith. It has given them control of their story. This is so much the case that today it is difficult to find histories of the church or biographies of its leaders not written by Latter-day Saints. Outsiders can charge that it has made the Mormons insular, but it is also true that it has made them the heroes of their own narrative. It has kept their doctrines, their culture, their family ties, and their sense of corporate mission intact when other religious movements have died in a famine of heritage.

Blessed by advantages other religions have not enjoyed at their beginning, the Saints started their life as a church. They immediately grew new groups of converts in Pennsylvania and New York. Persecution arose. It was natural. The Saints had proclaimed themselves the only true church with the only true prophet serving the only true God. It should have come as no surprise outside religious leaders would be offended. The Saints marched on confidently. Joseph Smith had put them at the center of God's work through the ages. In a revelation he said he received soon after the birth of the Church, he declared, "All old covenants have I caused to be done away in this thing; and this is a new and an everlasting covenant, even that which was from the beginning."

Revelations such as this cut both ways. If God could speak to every man he could also speak in opposition to the Prophet himself. Dueling prophecies were not unknown. Within months of the LDS Church's founding, Oliver Cowdery rebuked Smith for his revelation about Priests by saying, "I command you in the name of God to erase those words that no priestcraft be amongst us." Smith didn't back down and offered a counter-revelation: "Behold, I say unto thee, Oliver . . . no one shall be appointed to receive commandments and revelations in this Church, excepting my servant Joseph Smith, Jun., for he receiveth them as Moses. And thou shalt not command him who is at thy head, and at the head of the Church." Cowdery caved in and this left Smith the virtually unquestioned prophetic voice among the Latter Day Saints.

The Church continued to expand, planting still more "works" and starting a mission to the Indians, and this brought them in contact with Sidney Rigdon, a Baptist minister in Ohio. A powerful evangelist and a man ever in search of the pure, millennial people of God, Rigdon was volatile and mystical to the point some thought him imbalanced. He had been disillusioned with much that passed for true religion—even in the "restoration movement" that sought to reestablish the pristine New Testament "patterns"—and when LDS missionaries introduced him to the Book of Mormon, he was sure he had discovered the true church of Jesus. A month later, he and his entire congregation had been baptized as Mormons.

When Rigdon met Smith, it was a converging of complementary souls. Rigdon was thirty-seven, well educated, eager to be of influence among a holy people, and easily impressed with supernatural things. Smith was twenty-five, uneducated, eager to prove himself, and in search of followers. Rigdon's church was a ready-made congregation farther west and Smith began to believe that Rigdon's town of Kirtland might be a strategic base for the Lord's work out West. His Saints were not pleased with the idea at first, believing that Smith had come under Rigdon's sway. Then, as would often happen, prophecy prevailed. The revelation came to "go to the Ohio" for "there I will give you my law." The Prophet described "a land flowing with milk and honey, upon which there shall be no curse when the Lord cometh." Before he was done, he had included an instruction that was like many to come in leading to economic hardship for the saints: "And they that have farms that cannot be sold, let them be left or rented as seemeth them good."[4]

It was the beginning of a costly Mormon exodus. God's will, apparently, was that Smith's followers should uproot themselves whether they could sell their valuable farms or not and move the 300 miles west to Kirtland, Ohio. The blessing of God rested there. And a congregation of the likeminded awaited.

There were now 150 Mormons in Kirtland. If they had known what their faith would look like by the time Smith was done with it they might not have stayed. If a man had confidence in Joseph Smith as a prophet, he could conclude that Kirtland was where an open heaven granted abundant revelation. If he was skeptical of Smith, the same man might easily conclude that Kirtland was where that misguided mystic Joseph Smith lost all restraint.

He began by retranslating the Bible. This had nothing to do with reexamining the Hebrew, Greek, and Aramaic in which the Bible was originally written. In LDS jargon, to "translate" is to reinterpret by revelation, not by scholarship. Smith, with Rigdon at his side, asked the Holy Spirit to guide and then began rewriting the words of the Holy Book sacred to millions.

If it was not an act of obedience to revelation it was among the most arrogant, presumptuous deeds in the history of religion.

Smith and Rigdon translated by the hour and would report all types of spiritual experiences in the process, from great clouds of glory to manifestations so strong as to knock Rigdon out of his chair and almost unconscious. By the time this translating was done, thousands of verses were reworked. Not surprisingly, in every case Mormon doctrine was confirmed. Smith even wrote himself into the book of Genesis: he was a "choice seer" whose name would be Joseph "after the name of his father."

During this work Smith came to believe that there must be different levels of heavenly reward since every man would be judged by his works and not all men could be judged alike. On the authority of yet another revelation, Smith started teaching that there are "three degrees of glory." The "celestial" kingdom was for those who believed aright and kept the commandments. The "terrestrial" was a less exalted state but it allowed those who did not believe but who were "honorable" to repent and ascend to the "celestial" eventually. And the "telestrial" kingdom was for the truly wicked who would ultimately be redeemed by Christ himself at the last resurrection. Only those who denied the Holy Spirit after having once known him and who then gave themselves to Satan would be cast into hell. It was not quite universalism—the idea that all men will ultimately be saved, an idea gaining popularity in Smith's day—but it was close. It was also far from what the Book of Mormon taught about a lake of fire and brimstone, language borrowed from the Bible that Smith was just then rewriting.

The Prophet was far from done. He claimed to have revelation of a conversation between God and Moses that had failed to make it in the Bible. He also had a revelation of a lost book of "Enoch" and a fragment of Scripture buried by the apostle John. He had still another revelation establishing the offices of high priest and patriarch. The Lord talked to him about "stakes" and "wards," the varying administrative divisions of the Church. When Smith's wife, Emma, complained of tobacco stains on her floor after elders' meetings, her husband had the revelation called "The Word of Wisdom," forbidding "strong drink, wine, tobacco and hot drinks"—later interpreted as coffee and tea. By 1835 when he first published *Doctrine and Covenants*, there were 138 recorded revelations in its pages and these were not all he had received.

The very next year he claimed visitations by Moses, Elias and Elijah. He also instituted the doctrine of "sealing" by which families were bound together for all eternity. This applied to both living family members and the dead. There were other revelations, other doctrinal innovations. They seemed unending. LDS historian Richard Bushman wrote of this time, "Revelations came like water from an inexhaustible spring." By the middle of 1840 he was baptizing his people for the dead in the Mississippi. Already he was involved in one of the most embarrassing incidents of his prophetic life—the "translation" of the Book of Abraham, as we shall see.

He was creating the Church of the Saints and he was doing it on the power of his revelations. To understand how this was possible requires understanding one of the most central ideas of the LDS faith: progressive revelation. This is simply the belief that no revelation is final. There can always be new truth revealed from Heavenly Father and this new truth overwrites truth revealed before. Mormon truth is not to be found in a definitive, once-and-for-all scripture. Instead, scripture is constantly being revealed through prophets and anointed men. This is how Smith was able to rewrite the meaning of Mormonism time and again through revelation and there is no example of this so clear as that of polygamy.

It will probably come as a surprise to many outside the Church that the Book of Mormon does not teach polygamy. Instead, it teaches monogamy—the "one wife" principle:

> And it came to pass that Riplakish did not do that which was right in the sight of the Lord, for he did have many wives and concubines. (Ether 10:5)

> Behold, David and Solomon truly had many wives and concubines, which thing was abominable before me, saith the Lord. . . . Hearken to the word of the Lord: For there shall not any man among

you have save it be one wife; and concubines he shall have none. (Jacob 2:24, 27)

Behold, the Lamanites . . . they have not forgotten the commandment of the Lord which was given unto our father—that they should have save it were one wife, and concubines they should have none, and there should not be whoredoms committed among them. (Jacob 3:5)

Clearly, had the Book of Mormon been the final word on marriage, polygamy would never have existed among the Latter-day Saints. However, progressive revelation rules in Mormonism. And Joseph Smith never ceased to have revelations.

He had already become convinced of polygamy as God's will years before he made his convictions public, probably around 1831.[5] More than a decade later, in 1843, he issued the famous revelation that called Mormon men to take more than one wife, a revelation that appears in one of the official LDS books, *Doctrine and Covenants*, to this day.

Verily, if a man be called of my Father, as was Aaron, by mine own voice, and by the voice of him that sent me, and I have endowed him with the keys of the power of this priesthood, if he do anything in my name, and according to my law and by my word, he will not commit sin, and I will justify him.

Let no one, therefore, set on my servant Joseph; for I will justify him; for he shall do the sacrifice which I require at his hands for his transgressions, saith the Lord your God.

And again, as pertaining to the law of the priesthood—if any man espouse a virgin, and desire to espouse another, and the first give her consent, and if he espouse the second, and they are virgins, and have vowed to no other man, then is he justified; he cannot commit adultery for they are given unto him; for he cannot commit adultery with that that belongeth unto him and to no one else.

And if he have ten virgins given unto him by this law, he cannot commit adultery, for they belong to him, and they are given unto him; therefore is he justified. [6]

This proclamation was a bombshell. Smith knew it would be. He had already shared the revelation with his leaders some years before and it had not settled well with them. When Brigham Young heard this new part of God's plan, he said, "It was the first time in my life that I desired the grave, and I could hardly get over it for a long time. And when I saw a funeral, I felt to envy the corpse its situation."

But Smith wasn't through innovating. Either because he genuinely believed it to be God's will or because he was using religion merely to acquire women, he eventually joined his

new doctrine of polygamy to the doctrine of celestial exaltation. In other words, having multiple wives became essential to
achieving the highest level of salvation. As he told one teenage
girl he wished to wed, "If you will take this step, it will ensure
your eternal salvation and exaltation and that of your father's
household and all your kindred."

We see, then, the progression on the topic of polygamy
that is in keeping with the Mormon understanding of how
God works. Early Mormons practiced monogamy because it
was what the Book of Mormon taught. Then the Prophet had
a revelation. Polygamy became God's will. Then, another revelation. Polygamy is not only God's will, but it is essential for
the highest level of salvation. This was what most Mormons
believed for nearly half a century.

Finally, in 1890, another revelation came, this time to President Wilford Woodruff. Speaking as all Mormon presidents
do—in the office of "prophet, seer and revelator"—Woodruff declared polygamy at an end. He later said his revelation
was attended by a vision. Polygamy was no longer God's will.
Woodruff's famous "Manifesto" on the subject became part of
Doctrine and Covenants in 1908.

As LDS president Ezra Taft Benson declared years later,
"A living prophet trumps a dead prophet." What God reveals
today outweighs what God has revealed in the past. If Mormons
did not believe this, they would not have adopted a whole host
of doctrines which are now vital to their faith but which are
nowhere to be found in the Book of Mormon. These include

baptism for the dead, eventual exaltation to godhood, celestial marriage, eternal progress, a multitude of gods, varying levels of heaven, Temple ceremonies, and avoiding tobacco, caffeine, and alcohol—to name just a few.

Each of these came through revelations to Joseph Smith. He was either the prophet of God Mormons believe him to be or he had learned to manipulate a religiously overheated people by expressing his will as the will of God. Either way, he was unleashing forces that would bedevil his spiritual descendants for generations.

And what of Smith's wife? Emma Smith had suffered much, probably much more than anyone outside her home could know, and she would endure much more before her life with Smith was done.

Emma's entire history with Joseph Smith was costly. Marrying him had estranged her family and then drawn the animosity of neighbors and friends when the appearances of Moroni became known. Some souls are able to sustain the bombardment of negative opinions. Emma was not. The criticisms stung, the hatred filled her with fear. She begged Joseph to return to tilling the soil even after he began translating the famous plates.

She was unprepared for it all. There were the debt collectors she would probably have endured anyway in a life with

Smith but she never did get used to clergymen calling her an anti-Christ or newspapers calling her a whore. She never made peace with her father-in-law being in jail or her husband being on trial for all the world to see—and more than once. She knew that a Quaker to whom her husband owed money promised to forgive all debt if Joseph would just burn his copies of the Book of Mormon. Emma may secretly have wished he had taken the deal.

As one historian has said, "She had seen no plates and heard no voices."[7] She endured hardship as though she had. During one seven-year stretch she lived in four different towns relying largely on the kindness of friends. She had to flee mobs, authorities, and even disillusioned members of her own faith.

Her sufferings were particularly horrible because of the deaths she endured. Her first child died the day he was born. Emma barely lived through it both because of her physical trauma and for her grief. Then she became pregnant with twins. They also died. Soon after, she and Joseph took in a pair of twins whose mother had died giving them birth. Emma loved them as her own and then one of them died as well. In time she would have healthy children and they would live well into old age, but six of the ten children she had while her husband was alive were either stillborn or died in their first eighteen months.

Emma also endured the displeasure of her husband— and apparently of her husband's God—because she hesitated about some of Joseph's revelations. Most husbands upset with their wives would say so in private. Joseph Smith spoke to Emma in prophecies that lived in print—and as scripture—for generations.

> Emma Smith, my daughter . . . thou art an elect lady whom I have called. Murmur not because of the things which thou has not seen. . . . And the office of thy calling shall be for a comfort unto my servant, Joseph Smith, Jun., thy husband, in his afflictions with consoling words, in the spirit of meekness. . . . And thou needest not fear, for thy husband shall support thee from the Church . . . cleave unto the covenants thou has made. Continue in the spirit of meekness and beware of pride. Let thy soul delight in thy husband.

There would be other prophecies directed at her and some would threaten destruction if she did not obey.

Worse would come and when it did Emma would follow the dictates of her own heart and mind. Having seen all she had—having endured what few other women could have endured—she knew what was amiss and how men could mistake their wishes for the will of God. Never did she dishonor her husband. Yet in later years she was also unable to admit some of the indignities she had endured. It had all simply been too much.

CHAPTER 7

AMONG A PROGRESSING PEOPLE

Fuchs told me that the sunflowers were introduced into that country by the Mormons; that at the time of the persecution, when they left Missouri and struck out into the wilderness to find a place where they could worship God in their own way, the members of the first exploring party, crossing the plains to Utah, scattered sunflower seeds as they went. The next summer, when the long trains of wagons came through with all the women and children, they had the sunflower trail to follow . . . that legend has stuck in my mind, and sunflower-bordered roads always seem to me the roads to freedom.

—Willa Cather, *My Antonia*

It was the worst day of his life. He still felt like he was in some nauseating, slow-motion dream. But this had really happened. And everyone knew. And his children would never recover. And now he was sitting in the dark in a friend's back bedroom unable to hold a thought together in his mind for even a few seconds, so great was the pain.

Megachurch pastors weren't supposed to feel this way. In fact, megachurch pastors were supposed to have great marriages with adoring wives who said only good things about their husbands. But that wasn't the kind of woman he had married. It had gotten bad through the years, though his public life had thrived, and finally she had become so insecure and bitter that she had filed for divorce.

So it had been announced to the church—badly. His friendships would never recover. He had agreed to move out of his home because his wife made noises like she wanted to see the marriage heal. She didn't. He knew it. But she had to keep up the charade.

So here he was, sitting in the dark and thinking thoughts he had talked others out of.

And the phone rings. It can't be any of his friends. He doesn't have any now. And it certainly isn't any of his fellow pastors in the area. That bunch of cowards pulls away from a man once the rumors start. They don't want to be collateral damage.

He answers.

"Doc, it's Jammer." This isn't the man's name. It's a tag he picked up in the navy. It also describes what he can do on a basketball court but it isn't fun to think about unless he's on your team.

"Hey."

"Doc, I heard. You know how far removed I am from all that but I just wanted to touch base."

"Well, you're the first one to call."

"You're kidding. I'm sorry. Hey, let me take you to lunch."

"Look, Jammer, I appreciate that but I need to say—and forgive me for just not caring right now—but it's never going to happen. I'm never gonna join you guys. You know what I think about all that."

"You think I'm calling to convert you?"

"Yeah. I'm down and you're taking your shot."

"Wow. Thanks for *that*. Look, idiot. I'm calling because we're friends. We don't have to go back to that. You think I'm in a cult and I think you're so ill-informed you should be embarrassed. But all I want now is to see if you can get a bite and talk."

"Jams, I appreciate it. I do. But let me have some time before . . ."

"Okay. Okay. I'll let you go. But just think about this. Donna and I want to offer our guest house. No one's there and you can stay as long as you want while you, whatever— rebuild. And I'll make you a promise—but only because you're so stupid about these things. We don't ever have to talk about religion. We aren't doing this to draw you into our nets. We just like you. Always have. Despite the fact—you know—you're an idiot."

"Man. What . . . Why would you do this?"

"Well, we checked in at Temple Square and they gave permission. And so I thought I'd call—"

"Shut up!"

"You're the one who taught that we're all robots controlled from Salt Lake City! Not me!"

There's a pause. This kindness is foreign right now. He's trying to stay . . . dry.

"Look, Doc. You think about it. No pressure. We, you know . . . we mean it. All of it."

"Only one call from any of my friends and it had to be you! No. No. I'm . . . I'm just playing. This means a lot. I'm pretty blown away, really. I just might take you up on it, Jammer. Thank you. When do I need to let you know?"

"Well, Donna and I are leaving Wednesday to rule some other planets for a while so if you could let us know by then that would be—"

"I thought you said we wouldn't talk about religion."

"We won't. But talking about what an idiot you are is a whole other thing. Prepare for abuse."

"I get it. Maybe I even deserve it. Thanks, man. I'll call you in a few days."

There is a case to be made that the Mormon people have often been better than their leaders, and better than the doctrines their leaders have given them. From the beginning men and women had been drawn to the Latter Day Saints, most of them, because they simply hoped for something more. They had seen the swirl of messy revivals and bickering churches and they had never really understood it. They had certainly never understood the big fights over out-of-reach doctrines. So they turned to something new.

It had all been pretty simple at the start. God was restoring a true church. No creeds. No professional clergy. No complicated doctrines. Just the pure gospel of Jesus and every man a priest if he was willing and the Holy Spirit near to do amazing things. It was really all most people wanted.

It seemed to a lot of the Saints that it stayed pure for a good while too. At first, it was exciting. God seemed to be speaking to his people. Directly. Forcefully. With no fancy words or human conditions. God was talking like a man would talk to a man—clearly and understandably. And there were miracles to confirm what he said, as well.

Then it changed. There had been plenty of revelations to start the church and these were welcome. But then the Prophet had a revelation that everyone should uproot themselves whether they could sell their property or not and move to Ohio. It was hard for most folks but the Prophet said God commanded. Then the Bible got retranslated and the three degrees of glory came in a revelation and soon the Prophet was moving faster than most folks could understand. Revelations came in torrents—about a conversation between God and Moses and the real story of Adam and Eve and the life of Enoch and the exact location of the New Jerusalem. Before most Saints had moved to Ohio from New England, the Prophet was already talking about a new holy place in Missouri. He had so many revelations about church positions and structure that

the true Church became as complex as any of the denominations God called an "abomination."

It also started to get petty. The Prophet had revelations to
calm his wife and to have the saints build a house for him and to
shut down anyone who opposed him. He had special prophecies for his friends and an unusual amount of revelations about
money. He even said God told him everyone should sign their
property over to the Church and the bishops would give back
only what each one needed to live on. The Prophet grandly
called this "The United Order of Enoch." "Behold," came the
requisite revelation, "thou shalt consecrate all thy properties,
that which thou has unto me, with a covenant and a deed which
cannot be broken and they shall be laid before the bishop of my
church." Legal forms were provided. The arrangement didn't
last long. Then came the decree that some of the best things
in life—alcohol and coffee—were not God's will. It was disappointing to hear but no one dared oppose "Moses."

Then came the rumors. The Prophet was having an affair.
His leaders, some of whom had been with him from the beginning, thought he was a false prophet. His own brother got in a
fist fight with him. Some even said he was secretly married to
more than one woman.

Then it got strange. In July 1835, a peddler named Michael
Chandler wandered into the holy city of Kirtland, Ohio, and
had among his wares four Egyptian mummies and some papyri.
The Prophet, ever intrigued by things Egyptian and the hint
of dead languages, purchased it all for $2,400, a huge sum at

the time. He determined to "translate" the papyri—initially through actual linguistic work and then, finally, by revelation—and it was not long before he confidently announced that they contained lost writings of the patriarch Abraham.

The "Book of Abraham" that resulted was filled with new doctrines. There were many gods and they did not create the world. They "organized" matter that already existed. Abraham was an astronomer and knew that the planet "Kolob" was nearest the throne of God. In a novel interpretation that would haunt the Latter-day Saints for generations, the Prophet portrayed all Egyptians as descendants of Ham—the cursed son of Noah who, if racist folklore were believed, had black skin. On this slim basis, black people were denied the priesthood and access to the Temple. What suffering and humiliation came from this fiction, particularly when proclaimed by a Prophet of God.

It was all hard to understand. The idea that a peddler just happened to wander into an Ohio town carrying the 4,000-year-old writings of Abraham defied even the most active imagination. But it didn't take imagination to have doubts. Unlike the golden plates, which the angel Moroni took to heaven, these papyri stayed on earth and were later studied by experts—every one of whom said they were not what the Prophet claimed. They were simply funeral papyri of the kind Egyptians routinely placed in graves. Thousands have been recovered through the years. But the Church took the Book of Abraham as scripture.

It left being strange and became destructive. In 1836, the Prophet started a bank to help deal with all the Church's debts.

The very next year one of the worst depressions in American history occurred and lasted six years. Bankruptcy spread like a forest fire and the Prophet's bank closed, leaving only creditors' demands. Lawsuits were filed, many left the Church, and one man recalled that "there were not twenty persons on earth that would declare that Joseph Smith was a prophet of God."[1]

Before the end came, the Prophet urged the people to three different holy locations. Cruel persecution attended nearly every step and this prompted the rise of a militia of the "Danites" that grew in time to the largest army in the region. The Prophet loved it. He had himself been named lieutenant general and began wearing a uniform complete with sword, epaulets, and ostrich feathers. This was just a year before he announced his revelation about "plural marriage," or polygamy, which he had secretly been practicing for more than a decade.[2] An accompanying revelation assured his wife she would be destroyed if she didn't cooperate.

Opposition intensified against the Church but it didn't help that the Prophet kept marching his Danites around at full, intimidating strength, that he declared himself a candidate for president, and that his secret Council of Fifty named him "King, Priest, and Ruler over Israel on Earth." All the while he was still inventing his religion. In a single sermon from this time, he established the doctrine of a plurality of gods, of eventual divinity for the Saints themselves, of God having a physical body, and of God once being a man.

He was shot to death in 1844 while in a Carthage, Illinois, jail. He had surrendered to authorities only to be treacherously murdered, yet he was arrested because he ordered the destruction of an opposition newspaper—published not by gentiles but by disillusioned Saints.

When leadership passed to Brigham Young, the Church came no closer to the purity of her original purpose. He was converted to the faith in 1832 and immediately fell in among a branch of Mormons who extolled speaking in tongues. Young joined them and he quickly gained a reputation for the practice, which he sometimes performed before astonished gatherings. Some thought it was devilish. When Young met Joseph Smith and spoke in tongues for him, the Prophet declared it "the pure Adamic language." On the strength of such affirmations, Young rose quickly among the Saints.

He was hardworking and trustworthy and gave evidence of administrative gifts. It did not hurt that he was blindly loyal to Joseph Smith. When confronted with charges Smith was immoral, Young declared, "If he acts like a devil, he has brought forth a doctrine that will save us, if we abide by it. He may get drunk every day of his life, sleep with his neighbor's wife every night, run horses and gamble. . . . But the doctrine he has produced will save you and me and the whole world."[3]

He served the Mormon cause with herculean efforts— leading beleaguered Saints out of Missouri, pioneering the faith in England, and, of course, guiding the Mormon trek West— but he also encouraged doctrines and practices which long damaged his Church. He made a virtue of lying, which some Mormons called "Lying for the Lord" and which a leading LDS scholar has called "theocratic ethics." Young once boasted, "We have the greatest and smoothest liars in the world."

He could be violent. He pledged to avenge the death of Joseph Smith, he ordered castration as punishment for a number of misdeeds, and he spoke of killing men simply because they had no religion. He called himself a dictator who lived above the law and was sure "all hell" could not remove him.

He, like the Prophet, could also get weird. He urged siblings to marry. He was sure that the sun and the moon were inhabited. He also taught that Adam and Eve came from another planet and that Jesus was not conceived by the Holy Spirit but was "begotten in the flesh" by Adam and the Virgin Mary. He said he would feel as good about killing a row of criminals with a cannon as he would baptizing a convert. He also said that there were sins the blood of Christ couldn't cleanse but that could be atoned for by spilling the blood of the guilty. He stunned even Mormons by saying he did not know half of his wives.

He was, like the Prophet, gifted, strange, boastful, violent, maddeningly mystical, maddeningly misguided, and sometimes perverse.

This brings us back to the Mormon people, the true heroes of the Mormon tale. What did they do under such quixotic, often unsteady leaders?

They suffered. They sacrificed. They labored.

They followed the Prophet from place to place though some suspected his revelations. They erected model cities, built glorious Temples, and organized nearly every kind of enterprise—schools, relief societies, missionary societies, immigrant funds, businesses, dances, orchestras, theaters, and one of the most dramatic relocations of a people in American history.

They also died. Six hundred fell dead in the first winter of the western trek. Several hundred more died of starvation and hypothermia while trying to pull handcarts through snow to reach Salt Lake City in 1856. They were slaughtered in places like Haun's Mill, where a mob of 200 attacked thirty-eight men and boys, killing seventeen of them. One girl who witnessed the affair was haunted for the rest of her life by the sound of the dead being dropped into an unfinished well. The assault drew sanction from an extermination order issued by Missouri's Governor Lilburn Boggs—"the Mormons must be treated as enemies, and must be exterminated or driven from the State if necessary"—the only extermination order ever issued against a religion in American history. It was not rescinded until 1976.

They experimented with communal living and developed sophisticated relief and church welfare programs. During the Great Depression, President Roosevelt extolled their efforts as a model for the nation. They governed, educated, constructed, policed, lobbied, and worshiped as a community, as a people with a life in common.

This is what their experience produced, often despite their leaders and despite doctrinal oddities. They became a people. Even if their Prophet was a liar and their doctrines proved mere fantasies, on earth and in this life they became a people who, in striving to progress and achieve, became exceptional. It is the beginning of all the virtues we have surveyed, the virtues that made it possible for them to move from sect to influence in American society.

This is more than poetry, sentiment, or LDS spin. Spend time with students at Brigham Young University and the power of belonging to a people fashioned through rugged experience surfaces quickly. A junior political science major tells you some of her ancestors died on the Great Trek. The emotion in her face is as though it happened yesterday, she feels so a part of her people's past. Challenge another young woman, a senior premed major, about why she believes as she does and she will mention the death of a relative—six generations ago!—at Haun's Mill as though it is such an obvious basis for her faith that she is surprised anyone should fail to see it. It is impor-tant to remember that these two students are of a generation that has a difficult time placing the Civil War within a fifty-year period and nearly a third of which are unsure about what country Winston Churchill led. History may not seem near to their peers. It is ever present for most young Latter-day Saints.

Even those episodes in their heritage that outsiders might think embarrassing are understood to have made the Saints what they are. Non-Mormons might speak of polygamy with disgust and derision. In BYU professor Grant Underwood's deft hands, LDS students come to see their Church's season of encouraging plural marriage as part of Heavenly Father's plan. That season of tumult and spite set the Saints apart from society, called them to a costly obedience, and granted them a sense of belonging that comes only to a persecuted people. Every experience of their history is understood to be redemptive in this way, even suffering needlessly under misguided leaders and enduring criticism for views they do not hold. It is all part of becoming, part of passing tests, part of being hammered into a people of God.

This sense of being part of a people moving unified through time is behind much of what passes for our present Mormon Moment. Glenn Beck cannot speak of his faith without tears because he has never felt such belonging, never felt so in place. It is a product of the Saints being a people. Mitt Romney is reputed to trust only a small circle of friends, most of whom are Mormons. It may not be a political virtue, but it is not surprising that a sixth-generation Latter-day Saint would feel more in tune with other Saints. They are a people. Who else has been asked about their undergarments so many times? Fellow Saints understand.

And be assured that current Senate Majority Leader Harry Reid feels closer to his Republican fellow Utah Senator Mike

Lee than he does to most members of his own party. Both are Mormons and Reid was Lee's home teacher years ago. Even without that personal shared history, the two have a shared history of faith that gives them a bond stronger than politics. And when Donny or Marie Osmond look helplessly at a reporter when trying to explain what is most important to them as Mormons, it is because they cannot put words to this all-encompassing, invisible bond that comes with being a Saint. It is simply too profound to explain, particularly in a thirty-second sound bite.

We come home to where we began: "There is a case to be made that the Mormon people have often been better than their leaders and better than the doctrines their leaders have given them." It is certainly true. The faithful will object because they have been taught that obeying their leaders is essential to salvation. We can let them object. What we can know from Mormon history, though, is that it is the Mormon people who have accomplished the greatness of Mormonism. They, in essence, have worked the Mormon Machine. They tithed. They sent their children to foreign lands knowing they would hardly speak to them for two years. They attended meetings and paid tuition and were devoted to family and visited homes and submitted to any of a dozen categories of authority and underwent the Temple rituals and were willing to be thought odd in a conformity-addicted society. Whatever the spiritual, eternal benefits of being a Saint, being part of a historic, surviving, progressing people is the underlying strength of what has made Mormons such a secular success. They have outstripped their leaders. They have outstripped their more extreme doctrines. They have fulfilled the conditions of their faith and it has made them achieve. Understanding this is the beginning of understanding—at a purely human, natural level—what allows Mormons to ascend as they have in American society.

CHAPTER 8

THE EARTHLY FRUIT OF FAITH

In building up the kingdom of God, I am decidedly for self, and so are you. If you wish to obtain wealth, power, glory, excellency and exaltation of every kind, be for God and truth, and he will give you more than your hearts can conceive of.[1]

—Brigham Young

It was 1885 and the young doctor at Number 1 Bush Gardens in Elm Grove was beginning to feel like a failure. There was certainly reason for him to think otherwise when he looked back on his life, but his disappointments made the good hard to remember.

Though his childhood was blighted by his father's drinking, wealthy uncles made sure he went to the finest schools. He had attended prep at Hodder Place and then gone on to Stonyhurst College. There was that year at the Jesuit school in Austria before he studied medicine at Edinburgh. He had even been published in the *British Medical Journal.* Who could see failure in this?

Recently, though, it had all started to go wrong. He had come south to open a practice with George Budd, a favorite classmate. It hadn't worked out. Within months they parted company and the distraught doctor set up shop on his own in Portsmouth. His office was handsome, the sign over the street distinguished, but patients simply did not come.

Books helped distract him. He loved to read and devoured most anything about history or religion. He also started to write. It had always been a passion. He wrote a novel called *The Mystery of the Cloomber* and then short stories like "The Captain of the Pole-Star," which he loosely based upon his time as a ship's surgeon. As much as he reveled in imagining other lives, publishers showed little interest.

Then he hit upon an idea. He had been reading about the rise of a new sect in America. The papers were full of their curious ways and he had devoured every book about them he could find. He began to see how he could weave some fact with a good bit of fiction to make for a good yarn. It wouldn't hurt that the story was right out of the headlines.

The scenes forming in his mind so inspired him that he wrote the entire novel in three weeks. This was early in 1886. He had decided to let the tale begin with some murders in London. Then he would move the action to America, to the western territory of Utah. There would be a troubled wagon train and only two people, a man and a little girl, would survive. They would be at death's door when a huge party of Mormons— it was the name the papers used for that new American cult—

would rescue them. They would live with these "Saints" as father and daughter until the girl became a young woman. Then the story would begin to turn. Because these Mormons believed that every man ought to have numerous wives—it was God's will and the way to salvation—two men would want the girl as their next wife. But they would be older and eager only for social position. They would have no thought of love. There would be another young man who was not a Mormon and who did love the young woman. She loved him too, though she knew the Mormons would never allow her to marry a "gentile."

In time, the father, the young man, and the girl would try to escape. Mormon militia would intervene, kill the father, and marry the girl off to one of the scheming old polygamists. The young woman would not be able to survive it, a loveless life in a Mormon harem, and would die "of a broken heart" only a month later. The young man would know his duty: hunt the conspiring rascals down and kill them. This, eventually, he would do—in London, late in 1881.

When the novel was done, the doctor knew he had something special. It was certainly his best work. He began showing it to publishers and was ecstatic when Ward Lock & Company said they were interested. And they would pay! Twenty-five pounds for full rights!

The book was published in 1887 to mild sales but good reviews. The publisher commissioned another, and soon the public began paying attention. The doctor wrote more tales using the same lead characters and, in time, both the author and his intriguing mystery stories were beloved around the world.

There was something the doctor had done in writing this first successful novel, though, that haunted him all of his career. He had been hard on the Mormons. He had made them vicious and cold, held in check by a murderous band called the "Danites." They forced people into their religion with pronouncements like "Brigham Young has said it, and he has spoken with the voice of Joseph Smith, which is the voice of God." Though there were respectful comments—"the Latter Day Saints were as busy as the bees whose hive they have chosen for their emblem"—the Saints were portrayed as sinister and oppressive. "Not the Inquisition of Seville, nor the German Vehm-gricht, nor the Secret Societies of Italy," the novel confidently declared, "were ever able to put a more formidable machinery in motion than that which cast a cloud over the State of Utah." It was a society in which "every man feared his neighbour, and none spoke of the things which were nearest his heart." As the doctor's ever popular adventures blanketed the world, so did this particular view of Mormons.

Decades later in 1923, the doctor—by then a celebrated figure—launched a lecture tour in the United States. One of his appearances was held at the Mormon Tabernacle in Salt Lake City, Utah. Not everyone was pleased. The author's children were traveling with him and they were terrified. They had believed what they read in their father's book and most of what the papers back home had to say about the Mormons. Their nanny even told them they would likely be kidnapped once their train entered Utah. And some of the Mormons themselves weren't thrilled. A letter to the *San Francisco Chronicle* complained that the British doctor had "a lot of gall to take Mormon money when he attacked us so bitterly in his book."[2]

The evening at the Tabernacle went off without incident. A high-ranking Mormon introduced the famous author, the auditorium was packed, and the speech delighted everyone. The author later spoke of his "great respect for the Mormons, who treated me very liberally" and of "the friends whom I left behind in Salt Lake City." Yet, he never offered an apology for the way he had described the Saints in his first novel nor did he explain why he had depicted them so darkly. Many Mormons had hoped for it. His words had damaged them everywhere his book went.

In 1991, decades after the world-famous doctor and author had died, his seventy-eight-year-old daughter tried to explain. "Father would be the first to admit that his . . . novel was full of errors about the Mormons." He had "relied on anti-Mormon works by former Mormons because he believed these accounts to be factual." The Mormon leader who introduced the author at the Tabernacle those years ago also agreed. He remembered that the famous man had privately "apologized for that, you know. He said he had been misled by writings of the time about the Church."

The world would hardly know of this apology, though. It would know only the popular novel and its ominous portrayal of the Latter-day Saints. And it is a portrayal that is likely to live on for some time, probably as long as men read books. For the young doctor who became a famous author was Sir Arthur Conan Doyle and the novel he wrote was entitled *A Study in Scarlet*. It is the novel that first introduced an unsteady sidekick named Dr. John Watson and a "consulting detective" named Sherlock Holmes.

In searching for the mechanisms of the Mormon ascent from despised sect to national prominence, outsiders naturally look to the human, "real-world" benefits of the faith. A Mormon might well disagree. He might prefer to think that what the LDS have achieved is a blessing from their Heavenly Father. He might suggest that the Saints have succeeded because they have qualified and so they have been blessed with their current influence.

Yet the non-Mormon has no choice. The spiritual benefits of any religion are difficult to certify, even to describe. They must always remain in the subjective realm of faith and individual experience. Outsiders have to focus on the kind of mechanisms that we have already been identifying in this book: the human dynamics of the LDS system that tend to produce earthly fruit.

We have used the informal and kindly intended phrase "The Mormon Machine" to describe this system of LDS doctrines and duties. There is the centrality of the family, the priority of education, the calling to achieve, and the historic Mormon devotion to work, saving, the free market, and even divine law—like the US Constitution. We have also pondered the value of the LDS heritage in making the Saints a "people," and we've seen how their beliefs tend to make them moral, given to service, successful in hierarchies, and eager for unity over dissent. All of this is of value in making devoted Mormons prosperous and influential.

There is more, though, and it takes us even closer to understanding not only how Mormons ascend but also what it is like to be a Mormon and what we can expect from their place both in our lives and on the national scene.

During the interviews conducted for this book, dozens of Mormons were asked what inspired them about their faith. There were, of course, the religiously charged answers about God's love and the Book of Mormon and even the Temple rituals. But quite a number of Saints explained how they are inspired by the personal examples of the religion's great leaders. Naturally, this met with a good deal of suspicion until one woman went further and said that she was inspired in particular by the character of Joseph Smith.

It would be nice to report that this announcement met with kindness and understanding. It didn't. A rolling of the eyes was more the tone and this prompted the woman to say, "Look, I understand you don't like the Prophet, but there are parts of who he was that even a Protestant would find inspiring." The phrase "even a Protestant" was the hook and this woman was immediately asked—interrogated really—for more.

Since Smith has come in for quite a bashing in these pages, it was pleasant to think there might be themes more endearing than golden plates and seer stones to ponder about his life. The woman said that humorous stories she was told about the Prophet as a child had always reminded her to stay light-hearted. She quipped that Smith was "not always just 'verily' and 'behold.'" This was intriguing, and it turned out that she knew what she was saying.

Apparently, Smith could be engaging at times. He was often described as having a happy, fun-loving manner that drew people to him. He was not the dry, serious religious type typical of his age. Not everyone was happy about this, though. When a wagonload of pilgrims rattled into Kirtland and saw Smith playing cheerfully with children in the street, they immediately turned around and went home. He didn't fit their mold.

Smith sometimes used humor to make a point and this has also endeared him to Saints. When he was explaining his doctrine to a visitor one day, the man objected that he did not want theology; he wanted a miracle: "If you perform such a one then I will believe with all my heart."

Smith replied, "Well, what will you have done? Will you be struck blind or dumb? Will you be paralyzed or will you have one hand withered? Choose what you please and in the name of the Lord Jesus Christ it shall be done."

The man protested, "That is not the kind of miracle I want!"

"Then sir, I can perform none; I am not going to bring trouble upon anyone else to convince you."

Our Saintly woman said that she also had been inspired by Smith's courage and here again there were indeed examples of his nerve that could—even for those who do not share his religion—instruct and inspire. One of these episodes occurred on the evening of March 24, 1842. While Smith was tending a sick child in his home, a mob of gentiles and disaffected Mormons gathered outside. It was not the first time this had happened. Smith knew that they had come to humiliate and perhaps even kill.

Emma saw them first and screamed, "Murder!"

The men burst into the house, dragged Smith into the yard, and then stripped and beat him. He fought back, kicking with his one free leg. A man from the mob shouted that if he kept fighting they would kill him. Smith stopped resisting and the men struck him several more times.

"Spare my life!" Smith shouted, perhaps appealing to former Church members he recognized among the mob.

The men had not come to kill him, though. They had come to humiliate. Quickly, skillfully, they tarred and feathered him. When they were nearly done they tried to force the tar paddle into his mouth. This could mean death so he twisted and fought. They put a glass vial of tar between his lips and he bit through it in order to close his mouth. The wrestling continued until, finally wearied, the mob rode off, leaving the Mormon Prophet naked, tar-covered, feathered, and nearly unconscious on the ground.

Smith returned to his house with the help of neighbors and when Emma saw him and mistook the tar for blood, she passed out. Friends spent the night pulling and scraping the tar from his skin.

The next day was Sunday. The Saints gathered for their usual meeting but there was no Smith. Some in the crowd expected he would never arrive. They had been part of the previous night's mob. Then, suddenly, Smith appeared. He was "scarified and defaced" but clean and nicely dressed. He strode briskly to the front and preached with passion, never once mentioning the attack. It was the kind of display that cowed his enemies and in the retelling framed the valiant vision of Smith we see depicted in worshipful paintings today.

This belief that LDS history has lessons for the soul apart from its spirituality could easily have been mistaken as the interest of a few interviewees had it not been for the fact most of the Saints pointed to scenes from their history as being important to them. They would speak of plates, angels, and the law of eternal progression if asked, but without prompting they pointed to the hardships of the Great Trek, or the sacrificed lives at Haun's Mill, or the genius involved in building a city in the Great Salt Lake Basin. They had stories about LDS relief efforts after Katrina and even inspirational tales about BYU athletes that they did not expect outsiders to know but which made some kind of difference for them every day of their lives.

Outsiders tend to view the history of the LDS Church as a hypermystical experience filled with peculiar ideas and sometimes even more peculiar people. It is helpful to know that some Saints carry mental images of Smith or Young or Monson (the current LDS president) or even Glenn Beck or one of the Marriotts that inspire them as a framed photo of Vince Lombardi might someone else. There is an impact of LDS history at a nearly nonreligious level that has served to encourage and motivate many of the Mormon faithful.

There is a "natural" and "earthly" emphasis in Mormon theology, as well, and this has also contributed to the successes many Saints have achieved.

This is one of the great differences between Mormon thinking and, for example, that of some Protestant Christians. It is easy for traditional Protestants to slip into a spiritual tension with this world, their earthbound lives, and even their bodies. A casual knowledge of their faith can lead them to believe that phrases like "friendship with the world is enmity with God" or "do not walk in the flesh" or "do not be conformed to this world" mean that they are never to plant themselves or "fit" completely in this life. This is the influence of neo-Platonism on Protestant theology but knowing this is no comfort when a man feels guilty about being in too much harmony with the world around him.

Mormon theology causes the Saints to see their lives in this world as similar to the life of their God and not too different from what their lives will be in eternity. The God of this world has a kind of body, according to Mormon doctrine. It is not physical like a human's body is but it is such "purified spirit" that it appears physical. He has all the human parts and he has passion. It's a good thing because he has a wife. They have affection, sex, children, and lives together on a plane that is physical-like. They don't float among the clouds. In fact, the God of this world, according to LDS theology, has a mother and a father. He's part of a family, he's creating children to continue in the family business—ruling worlds—and he often fulfills his will in very earthly ways. Jesus was born, for example, because this Heavenly Father had natural intercourse with Mary.

In other words, the spiritual at least parallels and often interweaves with earthly life. A devoted Mormon man doesn't see his wife as someone to appease but avoid, or his children as people he wishes would get out of his house, or his job as something he clocks into but then can't wait to escape. His eternal purpose is interwoven with his wife and his children. They are an eternal family dynasty that was assembled before any of them were born, in that other, prior world called "premortality." His job is the training ground and the proving ground for that eternity. When this man thinks about time with his children or sex with his wife or the challenges of work, he knows these are also features of his Heavenly Father's life as well as the life this man may live one day if he qualifies. He would never shove his children out the door. The meaning of his life can't be fulfilled without them. He needs to love his wife—he'll be doing it forever.

Many non-Saints are so put off by the doctrines described in the paragraphs above that they don't even want to think about how these beliefs play out in the lives of Mormons. Yet these very spiritual ideas produce very earthly results and this is part of the reason for the astonishing Mormon rise of recent decades. As one cable news commentator has insultingly put it, "Mormons have goofy, mystical ideas that produce wonderful, earthly success." It may be unfair. It may be heresy. The LDS may even be a cult, as some have alleged. None of this changes the fact that Mormon spirituality not only makes the Saints feel perfectly in place in this life but it also embeds in them priorities and disciplines that lead to earthly progress of nearly every kind.

The inspiration Mormons draw from their history—even at a natural level—and the way their spirituality enhances their material well-being is experienced by most outsiders through one of the most effective tools the Latter-day Saints have:

celebrity. Mormons may have won souls through what they call "missions" but they have won social acceptance largely through the appeal of popular, successful Mormon personalities.

This probably began with a very controversial figure in American political history: Reed Smoot. There could hardly have been a man more thoroughly Mormon. He was born in Salt Lake City in 1862. His father was a Mormon pioneer, a Mormon elder, and the mayor at various times of both Salt Lake City and Provo. The elder Smoot had even officiated at the Mormon Temple in Nauvoo, Illinois.

Reed Smoot followed a distinctly Mormon path. He attended Salt Lake City public schools, went to college at the University of Utah, and then attended what was then Brigham Young Academy. He also became a Mormon apostle. In 1902, with the approval of the Church, he ran for a US Senate seat and won. This is when the political firestorm hit.

The Saints were still very unpopular in American society at that time. The Church had only banned polygamy a decade before but many Americans thought the practice secretly continued. They were right. There was also a popular rumor that Mormons took a secret oath against the United States out of bitterness over the death of Joseph Smith, the invasion of Utah by federal troops, and all the other indignities they had suffered.

Smoot's confirmation hearings became a circus that lasted four years. The Saints were put on trial with every myth and slur fully aired. Temple rituals and multiple marriages and blood oaths were all investigated with bias and an eye to the press by politicians hoping to establish reputations. When all was done, the Senate committee conducting the hearings voted against Smoot's confirmation. Thankfully, the full Senate over-ruled and Smoot took his seat in 1907.

Then, it happened. Nothing. President Theodore Roosevelt publicly celebrated Smoot's confirmation. The American people turned their attention to other matters. Mormons did not launch a coup and Smoot served in the US Senate until 1933. He was an effective statesman for both his country and his Church. In time, he chaired the Senate Finance Committee and served on the Senate Appropriations Committee, making him one of the most powerful men in the nation. His name will likely live as long as the Smoot-Hawley Tariff of 1930 is taught in schools. The bill is credited with exacerbating the Great Depression, proving that economic folly was not the province of the Protestant establishment alone. As Kathryn Flake has concluded in her masterful *The Politics of American Religious Identity: The Seating of Senator Reed Smoot*, "In sum, it can be said that the Mormon Problem was solved finally because the Mormons had figured out how to act more like an American church, a civil religion; the Senate, less like one."

Though it had occurred through an ugly process, Smoot became the first American Mormon celebrity—of sorts. The visibility and respect he commanded served to change minds about the Saints. It was a beginning.

Others would follow. There would be more LDS politicians—like Ezra Taft Benson, secretary of agriculture in the Eisenhower administration, and J. Reuben Clark, who was appointed US ambassador to Mexico in 1930. A Mormon woman became California's poet laureate in 1915. Her name was Ina Coolbrith, and she was Joseph Smith's niece. Her mother had been one of Smith's plural wives. It didn't matter. She was simply good at what she did, as were hundreds of other Mormons who won awards or assumed positions of authority or accomplished worthy feats. A Mormon athlete named Alma Richards won a gold medal at the 1912 Olympics and another named Jack Dempsey took the World Heavyweight Championship title in 1919 and held it for seven years. Soon, it became commonplace for standouts like these to be Mormon. Americans stopped being concerned and started being impressed.

Through the years there were war heroes and popular LDS presidents and always there were star Mormon athletes who drew adoring crowds. None of this, though, matched the astonishing popularity of Donny and Marie Osmond in the 1970s. The brother-sister team took Mormon celebrity to new heights. Nearly every edition of the teen magazine *Tiger Beat* extolled the virtues of the Osmonds' deep-seated faith. Every joke, dance, and song on their hit television show won not just acceptance—that had long before been accomplished—but respect and even newfound interest. It led to the current "Mormon Moment," which is tribute to the power of celebrity in our media age. From Glenn Beck to Harry Reid, from

Mitt Romney to Stephenie Meyer, visible, successful, interesting Mormons are, in a sense, closing the deal for the American Saints: they are sealing once and for all in the popular
mind the understanding that the Latter-day Saints have gone
well beyond being mere presence on the American stage and
have instead achieved a stunning level of influence for their
numbers.

There is another dynamic of Mormonism that helps explain
the achievements of the Saints, and it is the hardships and disciplines required by their faith. This is "old school," low tech, and
uninviting for most Americans, but it is unquestionably among
the great earthly benefits of the Mormon theological system.

Being a devoted Saint is costly. An LDS member is expected
to tithe, attend meetings, serve his local stake or ward, devote a
night a week to a family meeting, attend conferences, and fulfill
responsibilities in a dozen possible roles. This demands disci-
pline, the willing sacrifice of free time and pleasure, organizing
skills, and devotion to a prescribed level of excellence. None of
this alone reaches "hardship" status but it is still an unusually
long list of demands given what other American religions ask.

In addition, Saints are asked to fast once a month and by
this is meant no food or water for twenty-four hours. It is not
starvation but it is far more fasting than most Americans ever
attempt. Jews are urged to fast one day a year, on the Day of

Atonement, and Christians have no universal fast days at all, though the season of Lent provides opportunity to surrender some enjoyment for the sake of indentifying with the sufferings of Christ. Only Mormons, of all the major religions, expect complete denial of food and water twelve times a year. This still cannot be put in the category of "hardship," but it is, certainly for most Americans, a serious and often unpleasant sacrifice.

The arena of sacrifice and hardship that is most aggressive within Mormonism and that has produced the most astonishing results is the two-year mission the Church expects of its young. This lonely, difficult, even dangerous experience has fashioned some of the most successful leaders and most effective representatives the Latter-day Saints have ever sent into the world.

There have been nearly a million LDS youth sent on missions. They range in age from nineteen to twenty-one. They spend up to three months at the Missionary Training Center in Provo, Utah, where they train during arduous ten-hour days. Once this training is done, the missionaries do not have any control over where they are sent. The LDS Quorum of the Apostles decides each missionary's destination. Fifty percent will go abroad. Once there, these youths will pay $400 to $500 a month for the privilege of living like the locals, spending the majority of their days handing out copies of the Book of Mormon and trying to win strangers to their faith. They will be teamed with another missionary their entire two years and will rarely have time alone. They will have one day a week of free time, but that day is also when washing and letter writing must be done. Perhaps most difficult of all, they will not go home for the entire two years and will only be allowed four phone calls to their parents during that time—one on each Christmas and one on each Mother's Day.

Save perhaps the demands of the Roman Catholic priesthood, there is hardly a religion that asks as much for as long a time. Yet precisely because these missionaries are required to give so much so young, they grow up quickly and they return home usually dramatically changed and ready to achieve.

The list of LDS corporate leaders and politicians who point to their mission experience as defining in their success is impressive. It includes Mitt Romney, who was almost killed in a car accident during his mission in France. There is also Stephen Covey; David Needleman of JetBlue; former ambassador and Utah governor John Huntsman; Kim Clark, once dean of the Harvard Business School; Gary Crittendon of CitiGroup, American Express, and Sears; and the list could continue for pages. Mormons are disproportionately represented as corporate CEOs and board members, in senior government jobs, in top university jobs, and among the nation's wealthiest. The LDS two-year mission is one of the reasons why.

Much of this is due not only to these two-year missions and what they produce in the missionaries' lives but also to the culture this vast effort creates among all Latter-day Saints. Sacrifice is valued, hardship is embraced, evangelism is central, and all of this changes how even little brothers and sisters back home perceive their lives. It is one of the most ingenious facets of the already amazing Mormon Machine.

Each of the features of Mormonism we have surveyed above—the ability to draw practical inspiration from the LDS journey, the earthly effect of Mormon spirituality, the power of celebrity, and the valuing of hardship—have helped to propel the Latter-day Saints to prominence. Laid alongside the elevating features of the faith we have already explored—the religious priority of achievement, family, education, work, the free market, heritage, networking, and the various other engines of the Mormon Machine—it is not hard to see why the duties and disciplines of the faith have led to the prominence the Saints now enjoy. It is not going too far to say that if these same values were lived by another people with no supernatural beliefs at all, there would still be earthly benefits to reap. This is not the message of the Saints, of course, but it is a message of their American journey.

CHAPTER 9

THE WORK UNFINISHED

I have more to boast of than ever any man had. I am the only man that has ever been able to keep a whole church together since the days of Adam. A large majority of the whole have stood by me. Neither Paul, John, Peter, nor Jesus ever did it. I boast that no man ever did such a work as I. The followers of Jesus ran away from Him, but the Latter-day Saints never ran away from me yet. [1]

—Joseph Smith

It is 4:30 in West Des Moines, Iowa, and on court number nine at Royal Racquet Fitness, Bill Monk and Daniel Cassidy are hitting the ball so hard it hurts the ears. Both are A-class players, both are fiercely competitive, and the two have been playing racquetball against each other for years.

Cassidy steps to midcourt to serve and calls the score: "13–12."

He fires a drive serve down the left wall to Monk's backhand. Monk barely gets his racquet on it, returns it to the ceiling, and then circles a backpedaling Cassidy to get out of the way. The ball comes high off the back wall and Cassidy intends to roll it out. He cocks the racquet in his right hand to his left shoulder and snaps it low and forward, turning his torso as he hits the ball. He feels a slight spark of pleasure knowing he has hit it well. But then, too early, he hears a "splat!" The ball has hit Monk, who knew how good Cassidy's backhand was and moved in too close to defend. Monk growls loudly. Cassidy knows how much this hurts, particularly in the small of the back. He winces in sympathy and stays in the corner out of the wounded man's line of sight.

"Man! That hurts!" Monk is hobbling around the court. He's been hit like this before. It stings like nothing else and bruises for months. His wife orders him to stop playing every time she sees one of the bluish-red explosions on his back.

"I'm so sorry, Bill. I didn't know you were close. Where were you going?"

"Oh, like this is my fault!" Monk says with a pained grin.

And then, in the teasing way the two have enjoyed for years, Monk says, "You know, if you keep hitting me with the ball you will never be the god over your own planet."

Cassidy doesn't miss a beat. "If I'm ever the god over my own planet, you *will not* be on it!"

They are famous for this. Cassidy is a Mormon stake president. Monk is the pastor of a Des Moines megachurch. The two are friends, have double-dated, and have played racquetball every week for nearly five years. The city paper even did an article on their friendship, highlighting their religious banter on the court. It was entitled "The Mormon and the Monk: An

Unlikely Friendship." The two have been an inspiration in the community.

Cassidy serves again. Monk returns it but drives the blue ball into the floor. It's 14–12. Cassidy does a beautifully lobbed Z-serve that comes off the side two inches from the back wall. Monk can't get behind it and the ball falls to the floor. Game over, 15–12.

Monk offers his hand. "Good game. Next time, though, I'd like to play you when I'm not mortally wounded."

Cassidy looks sheepish, apologizes again, and holds the door in the back wall for Monk to step through. They sit down on a bench just outside and start guzzling Gatorade. Making the distinct sounds of winded, aching, middle-aged men, they towel off while throwing their gear into their bags.

"Hey, I need to ask you something." Cassidy looks over at Monk and sees he is pulling some stapled pages from the side pocket of his Ektelon bag. "Someone sent this to me, and I have to say that as much as you and I have talked about LDS and everything, I didn't know this."

"What is it?" Cassidy asks, a bit confused by Monk's tone.

"Well, apparently the guy who sent this to me found a transcript of the Temple Endowment Ceremony on the Internet." Monk looks at his friend as though he expects Cassidy to know just what he means.

"Well, that's not likely. Those ceremonies are sacred. No one records them or writes anything down. You're probably looking at another one of those ex-Mormon website rants."

"I don't know, this seems pretty specific. And I tell you what, it doesn't paint a very complimentary picture of guys like me." Monk forces a smile but Cassidy sees that a shadow has come over his face.

"Now come on. We've been through this 'true church' and 'restored gospel' stuff before. You know what we believe. What's up?"

"Well, I have to say that I didn't know your ceremonies depict pastors like me as literally working for the devil. I mean, it's like we are all serving Satan for the money. Here, look at this."

Cassidy looks over the sheets from Monk's printer. Then he shakes his head and chuckles. "You know, you're an idiot." Monk isn't sure how to take this. Cassidy quickly starts talking again so there isn't time for his friend to misunderstand. "This is a transcript—I guess it's a transcript—but it's at least somebody's remembrance of the endowment ceremony as it used to be. Yes, they used to speak of non-LDS clergy as 'sectarian ministers' and they used to show them as working for the devil. But all that stopped in the 1990s. It isn't part of the ceremony anymore. And they stopped it because it was offensive to you guys, Bill. This is nothing at all. Really." He hands the papers back to Monk.

But Monk isn't appeased. "Look, take me seriously on this. I mean, you were in the Church in the 1990s. And here, read this. No, I'll read it to you. This guy called 'Sectarian Minister' has just been talking to Satan and now the apostle Peter is asking the dude what he thinks about Satan. Here goes.

> **Sectarian Minister:** *He is quite a different person from what he told me the devil is. He said the devil has claws like a bear's on his hands, horns on his head, and a cloven foot, and that when he speaks he has the roar of a lion!*
> **Peter:** *He has said this to deceive you, and I would advise you to get out of his employ.*
> **Sectarian Minister:** *Your advice is good; but, if I leave his employ, what will become of me?*

Monk stops and just stares at Cassidy, his eyebrows raised. This is such a break from their usual manner that Cassidy gets a little heated. "Look, I'm telling you this is old stuff. You might as well pick a fight with me about polygamy or Mountain Meadows or some of the other stuff we've talked over. Bill, I don't mind answering questions and neither do you, but don't pull stuff off the Internet and then pin it on me like it's something I believe."

"I'm not picking a fight, Cas. I just need to know. Just tell me that this isn't what the LDS thinks today. Tell me 'sectarian minister' isn't how you guys talk about me behind the scenes and that no one in the Church thinks guys like me are serving the devil!"

Cassidy has had it. His face is red, his eyes are wet, his movements quick and angry. He zips up his bag, throws the strap over his shoulder, and squares off to Monk.

"I won't be grilled. I'll talk to you about anything you want. I always have. But I'm not going to be interrogated like some criminal. Can I tell you nobody among the millions of Saints thinks these things? No, I can't. Maybe they do. It isn't part of our doctrine, though. I mean, Bill, you've been to my house for dinner. I've spoken to your staff. You really don't know what I think about stuff like this?"

There's a pause. Monk opens his mouth to speak, but Cassidy isn't done.

"Now, Reverend Monk. You answer something for me. Can you tell me that not one of all the thousands in your church thinks I'm in a cult? Can you tell me that no Evangelical thinks that our beliefs are 'doctrines of demons'? And then tell me this: no one—I mean not one of the people you pastor—thinks I'm going to hell and taking everyone in my stake with me? Really? No one?"

Monk says nothing. He can't. He knows it is all true. This is exactly what most of his people believe. And he's still steamed that Mormons think he serves the devil. He didn't know. The silence says everything.

Cassidy turns to go. As he walks out the door, he says over his shoulder, "I don't know if I'll be here next week. I'll let you know."

As in the vignette above—a true story, told by two friends who have now reconciled—the past sometimes steps into the present at inconvenient times, disturbing hopes for the future. Our response at that moment determines everything. We can ignore the urgings of the past and, by shutting our minds to what C. S. Lewis called "the clean sea breeze of the centuries," close ourselves off from wisdom. We can turn too much to the past in sentiment and nostalgia, and so lose the future. The wise path is almost always to hear the counsel of ages past and make the changes required, keeping the restrictions of the present and the demands of the future in mind.

It is not easy. There is little as disturbing to the human soul as change. Some say it is because we were callously thrust from the comfort of the womb once and so we spend the rest of our lives making sure something like it doesn't happen again. What we can end up fighting against is change of any kind and this means resisting growth. Winston Churchill helped us with this when he said, "To improve is to change; to be perfect is to change often."

In the years to come, there will be great shifts in the relationship between the Church of Jesus Christ of Latter-day Saints and the rest of American society. It can hardly be otherwise. Whatever happens in a single industry, political race, or media configuration, Mormons have reached critical mass. It means that their numbers have increased to the level and their "diaspora" has broadened to the extent that most Americans know a Mormon, like him or her, and want to know more—both of friendship and about the LDS faith. As the Pew Forum reported not long ago, "The large majority of those who know a Mormon (60%) express a favorable view of Mormons, compared with fewer than half (44%) of those who do not personally know a Mormon. And those who are acquainted with a Mormon are 11 points more likely than others to say that Mormonism and their own religion have a lot in common."[2]

This relational dynamic will merge with more culture-wide dynamics involving celebrity, politics, civil religion, and wealth to place the Latter-day Saints on a wider stage, under brighter lights, and with a larger audience than ever. It will mean change; perhaps, if they are willing, profound change. What is certain is that all will not continue as in recent decades.

This will at times be uncomfortable for the Saints but if they are familiar with anything it is certainly the price of change. They have changed doctrine, changed geography, changed generations of leadership, and changed their public face each more than once and they have not forgotten what is required.

To get a glimpse of how much change they have undergone, consider just the small matter of style. To watch an LDS conference on television is to see a great formal affair with dozens of elderly men sitting upon multitiered rows of seats and dressed in dark suits and often darker ties. There is order, decorum, gravitas.

Consider how this differs from the dedication of the Temple in Kirtland during the summer of 1836. It lasted for a week. There were a thousand worshipers. Another thousand stood outside. Hymns erupted spontaneously, as did "shouts"— the simultaneous yelling of phrases like "Hosanna to God and the Lamb with an Amen, Amen, Amen" or a simple "Hallelujah." Men felt the Holy Spirit's fire and saw visions which they roared out for the edification of all. Jesus had come with his angels.

Sidney Rigdon preached for two and a half hours. When Smith spoke, he prayed for a new Pentecost: "Let thy house be filled with a rushing mighty wind, with thy glory." He asked for all to be "clothed with salvation." He led shouts to God "sealed" by cries of "Amen, Amen, Amen." Finally he declared that the Temple was filled with angels.

This was followed by a young man giving an address in tongues. His name was Brigham Young. A second man interpreted what Young was saying for all the rest. The meeting was dismissed at 4 p.m. It had begun at nine that morning—seven hours earlier. Hundreds claimed to speak in tongues. Many said they saw angels and others witnessed pillars of fire. Words of prophecy were abundant. More than a few claimed to be healed. Before the week was over, Joseph Smith had met with Elias, Elijah, and Moses.

The next LDS Conference will not likely resemble this gathering in 1836. Change has occurred.

It is not hard to imagine some of the changes—perhaps for a while they will simply be questions—that these relational and cultural dynamics will press upon the Saints.

One will certainly be that of loyalty. This will be insulting to Mormons, given that they have been among the most loyal Americans of all. Yet they have to know that lurking behind all they do is the question of whether they have sworn undying loyalty to their Church in such a way that trumps their loyalty to their country. Vanderbilt University's Kathryn Flake quipped in her fine book on the Reed Smoot affair, that if Alexis de Tocqueville "had lived to see the Mormon kingdom, he probably would have been amused that the nation with the soul of a church had given birth to a church with the soul of a nation." Non-Mormons sense this nation-like nature of the LDS world and it makes them wonder what kind of hold it has on the devotion of each Saint. Perhaps more important, it makes them wonder what the Saints' religious devotion takes away from devotion of other kinds.

Another aspect of Mormonism that the Saints will feel pressured to change is their secrecy. Americans understand that some elements of the LDS faith are sacred—it is true of most all faiths—and that this means private and therefore secret. This is not the pressing issue. Many gentile bridesmaids have sat in the visitor's lobby of a Temple while their LDS friends completed their wedding ceremony inside. Clearly, the gentile bridesmaid was thought too much a stranger to be permitted inside. It stings a bit, but there is no record of enraged gentile bridesmaids storming the barricades between the lobby and the business end of the Temple. Most everyone understands and is deferential. Likewise, many a gentile executive has sent a gift to an LDS associate, offering best wishes after deeply meaningful ceremonies the gentile is not allowed to attend. This version of sacred has been honored time and again.

What we will likely have to bow is the version of sacred/secret that guards rituals in which Saints in positions of power receive revelations. Is it really to be the case that while a Mormon sits in the White House or as chairman of the Joint Chiefs or on the United States Supreme Court, he can receive a patriarch blessing or some other kind of prophetic download and no one is to ask who has said what to whom or how final the words are considered to be by the faithful?

When Sarah Palin was the Republican nominee for vice president in 2008, a video surfaced of her receiving prayer at a Wasilla, Alaska, Assembly of God church. Since it was a Pentecostal church, some on the video could be heard praying in tongues and others could be heard rebuking demons while Palin knelt next to an African bishop and received a prayer for wisdom. It was a prayer that could have been voiced in most any theologically conservative Christian church. It was all pretty tame, standard fare for the Pentecostal/charismatic stream of modern Christianity. No one thought much of it at the time.

When the video hit the Internet, there could not have been more of a reaction had Palin been caught having an affair. She was in the grip of an African "witch hunter," she had shown mental imbalance by speaking in tongues, she had disqualified herself for public office, and she had probably given some unknown offense to prevailing views of the First Amendment.

It was all absurd. There have been high-ranking Pentecostals in the US government for decades. Yet there was one matter Palin's critics had right: the American people do have the need and the right to know who is claiming to speak for God to those in public office. It was true of Reagan. It was true of Clinton. It should be true of every senior member of the US government. It will also need to be true of Latter-day Saints.

There is too the matter of intellectual accountability for what Mormonism claims. Certainly, no man has to give an answer for anything he believes in the United States. An American can worship whatever he wishes and never have to explain himself to another. That is our grand tradition. However, when that same man takes his faith into the public arena and asks that his beliefs affect the wider world, that faith is subject to some accountability. It is the same for the Latter-day Saints.

The LDS Church has pumped millions of dollars into the State of Hawaii of late. They are reaching to beleaguered and often bitter native Hawaiians with funding for scholarships, cultural centers, and the like. This is their right. However, they are basing their aggressive efforts on the assertion that seafaring Nephites sailed west from South America and became the ancestors of the Polynesian peoples. This not only makes native Hawaiians descendants of Hebrews but it also makes them, in some way, long-lost Saints. Now they must be brought back into the fold.

The result is that an already abused people are being lured by money into a view of history that is meant to supplant their own. Again, this is their right—both the natives and the Saints. But what facts are there to legitimize this absorption of a culture? Is there any evidence that the Nephites ever existed? Is there any evidence they were Hebrews? Is there any evidence that a native Hawaiian is descended from Hebrews? Is there any evidence that any people from South America became the natives of Hawaii? These are not questions that should go unasked and certainly not unanswered. The heritage of a great people is at stake.

The need is for answers that are very much like those the Church gives on other matters. Whatever virtue there was to the Mormon support for California's Proposition 8—a move against same-sex marriage—the Church was at least willing to offer an apologetic. When LDS public relations chief Michael Otterson was asked about the issue, he said clearly, "We are compelled by our doctrine to contend for the family." Then he offered extensive research to support the LDS view that the traditional family makes for a strong, prosperous society and preserves a culture through time. It is important that this same level of factuality and accountability is behind every public act of the Church.

The Saints should also expect that their doctrine and their beliefs about history will come under fresh examination. It will simply not be enough for a new generation—even a new generation of Mormons—that the faithful have a testimony, a mystical inner knowing, as confirmation of doctrines and claims for which the Church can produce no evidence. No one will care that the existence of Kolob goes unproven or that there is no evidence to support the assertion that Jesus and Mary Magdalene were married. These can safely remain in the realm of faith. But it will become increasingly embarrassing and discrediting to claim that a civilization existed in the western hemisphere for centuries and yet to be unable to produce any evidence that non-LDS experts would respect. It will not do to claim that Native Americans are descended from Hebrews when DNA evidence indicates otherwise. And after nearly 200 years of LDS history, surely there ought to be some shred of evidence for the existence of Reformed Egyptian which, again, non-LDS experts can affirm. To fail to provide such evidence would be something like more traditional Christians being unable to prove there was a Roman Empire when it is assumed on nearly every page of their New Testaments. If no evidence could be produced after 2,000 years, non-Christians would be just in concluding that the New Testament is not true—or at least not historically true, whatever its spiritual virtues.

The relationship between the Latter-day Saints and traditional Christians—Roman Catholics, Evangelicals, other Protestants, and the like—will also come under new examination. It will not be a pleasant experience for either side.

The Saints have made it clear they wish to be thought of as Christians and take great offense when Evangelicals call them a cult. Both are understandable. Yet it is time to move toward a greater honesty and sophistication on this matter than we have seen. The LDS Church was born in an announcement that all Christianity at the time was false. Joseph Smith offered another book as of equal authority with the Bible, then reworked the Bible in his own image—he inserted himself into the revised book of Genesis!—and then retooled Christian doctrines into a form Christians would not recognize. There was the "sectarian world" and there was the only Church of Jesus Christ. The worldview of the Saints offered no middle ground. A single sentence from Brigham Young makes the point: "Every spirit that confesses that Joseph Smith is a prophet, that he lived and died a prophet, and that the Book of Mormon is true, is of God, and every spirit that does not is of Anti-Christ."

What was a good Methodist or Baptist to do?

Some Saints will say that those days are over and that attitudes have changed. Perhaps. However, the Saints still win converts by telling them their Christian churches are displeasing to God. LDS missionaries still target the pews of

Christian churches and routinely troll the wake of Christian crusades, gathering up those souls stirred by religious excitement but not meaningfully connected or taught. LDS doctrine still includes the belief that only the LDS Church is pleasing to God, has authority, has the true gospel, and can fulfill Heavenly Father's will on earth. And, of course, only the LDS Church has the ordinances required for salvation.

When a Baptist says that the Saints are not Christians, he is referring to distinctions the Saints themselves have made. When he says that the Latter-day Saints are a cult, he should be wiser when he speaks publicly but he is normally using the word in its technical sense. The word *cult* can mean a deceived band of people led toward their destruction by a dynamic, manipulative leader. This is usually not what is meant of the LDS. However, the word used by an Evangelical or Christian conservative almost always means "an organization built upon a perversion or significant revision of traditional Christian doctrine." This is exactly what Smith, Young, and company intended and it is, by their own confession, what the LDS is.

It is time, perhaps, to follow the counsel of scholar Jan Shipps and to proclaim the Church of Jesus Christ of Latter-day Saints the "Fourth Abrahamic Religion" along with Judaism, Christianity, and Islam. Perhaps it is time to admit that public offense at the words *non-Christian* hides a two-sided battle for the definition of what Christian is. Perhaps it is time to admit what is true and is even said privately behind closed doors at Temple Square: the Saints never cared about being called Christian until it became necessary for influence in an American society with a Judeo-Christian memory.

Mormons are well able to navigate these currents of change. They are a creative, ever-adapting, inventive people, and they seem intent upon succeeding in the coming age of religious fascination and contention. However, they may be caught unprepared by what success in this just-dawning era will require. They cannot remain insular while a growing number of their members wield civic power. They cannot win trust without transparency. They will not win admiration without, as Jefferson wrote, "a decent respect to the opinions of mankind." They cannot forge the futures of people groups unless they first honorably address still unanswered questions about their own past. All of this will be demanded of them in the season to come. They will either refashion themselves in order to thrive in the modern world or a refashioning will be forced upon them by the persistent weight of American culture. To use the ancient words, they will either fall upon the rock or the rock will fall upon them.

When *Newsweek* magazine proclaimed, "No question the Church of Jesus Christ of Latter-day Saints is 'having a moment,'" the Saints understood that their new visibility was no brief appearance on a well-lit stage.[1] They are to be congratulated. They have, in a genuine sense, arrived. They have built a globally influential Church, produced one of the best universities in the world, organized unparalleled relief programs, and launched their members to stellar heights of influence, wealth, and fame. Their story inspires, convicts, and convinces. It is an American story. It is one of the great stories in the annals of religion.

For the Saints, this ascent is the blessing of Heavenly Father. It is the reward of obedience, the outworking of predetermined plans, the grace given to those proven worthy. We would expect of them little else.

For outsiders, though, there must be other ways to explain the surprising prominence of the Latter-day Saints. Respecting them as we may, we look beneath their supernatural claims and we find, once again, Joseph Smith. He founded their religion. He refashioned it by the force of his revelations for more than a decade after its founding. He is the guiding spirit in every Mormon heart to this day: "I believe that Joseph Smith is the true prophet of the true and living Church."

If we do not believe Smith was led by a Heavenly Father making his will known through the angel Moroni, and if we do not believe—as some do—that he was moved by evil spirits, then there is another view that might explain the rise of the Saints. It may be that while Mormonism was not the founding religion of America, it is a religion founded in America that evolved over time into a religion of America—a spiritualized version of all that ennobled the United States of Joseph Smith's day.

If Smith contemporaries like Isaac Hale and Alexander Campbell were correct, the Mormon Prophet created his religion out of the raw cultural materials of his age—the America of the Jacksonian period. Perhaps this explains, from a secular perspective, what Mormonism became. Perhaps Smith did indeed create the religion of the Saints from the visions of his own exceptional mind. Perhaps he suctioned up the worldview, the aspirations and the core values of the time in which he lived and spun from them a demanding religion that fashioned an exceptional people through costly doctrines, confrontation with the surrounding society, and spiritual passion.

If this is even partially true, it provides a most intriguing explanation of why the Church of Jesus Christ of Latter-day Saints has thrived as it has in American society. It may be that Mormonism is the American experience distilled. It may be that Joseph Smith had a gift for summarizing and systematizing that allowed him to create a religion out of the disparate parts of the early American experience. It is not hard to envision. Mormonism is, at heart, about progress, about ruling pristine territory, about the spiritual matrix of family, about the democratization of spiritual experience, about sacred ritual, about the elevating power of community, about a people escaping a corrupt world in the east to establish a holy community in the west, about a "land of liberty," about natives with a sacred heritage unknown to them, and about truths long lost and newly revealed. This is the religion of the Saints, but it is also the underpinning of the American dream. The two draw from much the same spiritual soil, extol nearly the same spiritual values, envision the same ultimate state—a family divinely empowered to rule a sacred land.

This view assumes an entirely non-supernatural view of the Mormon faith. It understands Joseph Smith as an ingenious man who completely imagined the religion he said he received by revelation. It also understands Smith as a manipulative deceiver who led his unsuspecting followers by constant revelations and by unceasing demands for sacrifice. It interprets the heartiness of the Latter-day Saints as a product of invented religious doctrines that have nevertheless fashioned a capable, ambitious people over time.

If this is true—if Joseph Smith created a religion of American cardinal principles for a people who lived them on American soil and by them ascend to unprecedented American success—then the "Mormonization of America" has only been possible because there was first the "Americanization of Mormonism." This is more than just a turn of phrase. It may be the hidden truth behind one of the few uniquely American religions and one of the most influential faiths of our time.

It would mean also that the earthly success of the Saints is replicable, that it occurred on the strength of principles the non-Saint may emulate. In this view, the Mormon distinctives would cease to be understood as distinct and would become instead principles of Americanism available to the willing of any faith. Perhaps for the non-Mormon, this is the meaning of Mormonism, the meaning of our present "Mormon Moment": that there are principles of material ascent available for any people, principles Mormons have lived well but which belong to all humankind.

What is certain is that this Mormon Moment will pass. But Mormonism and its influence will not. The faith of the Saints will be ever remaking itself through both revelation and adaptation to the times, but always its trajectory will be upward, always it will be progressing toward mystical ends and always it will be seeking to live out what it perceives to be its divine destiny on American soil.

Joseph Smith's Articles of Faith

Joseph Smith wrote the following thirteen articles of faith in 1842. At the request of John Wentworth, editor of the *Chicago Democrat*, Smith penned a brief history of the Latter Day Saints and concluded with these brief statements of Mormon doctrine.

Now remembered as the Wentworth Letter, it is significant for several reasons. First, it is one of the few systematic statements of doctrine from the Church's early history. Second, it contains language that sounds much like that of other historic creeds except that there are slight turns of phrase that reveal a break from traditional Christianity. Men are not sinners because of Adam's fall from grace but rather because of their own individual sins. The atonement of Christ is not all that is needed for salvation. It requires obedience to "laws and ordinances" as well. The Bible must be "correctly translated" in order to be the Word of God and only then does it share the status of the Book of Mormon. Finally, it is clear that these statements do not include everything that the Church of Jesus Christ of Latter Day Saints had accepted as true by 1842. There were numerous new doctrines contained in Joseph Smith's many revelations that were not included in these thirteen statements and there would be more before he died in

1844. Clearly, Smith wrote these statements with the intent of positioning his Church favorably in the mind of Christian America at the time.

To perceive the spirit in which these statements were offered to the world, it is important to include the paragraph that came just before these articles in Smith's letter to Wentworth. It reveals both the impressive expansion of the Saints around the world as well as Smith's defiance in the face of fierce opposition.

Our missionaries are going forth to different nations, and in Germany, Palestine, New Holland, the East Indies, and other places, the standard of truth has been erected: no unhallowed hand can stop the work from progressing, persecutions may rage, mobs may combine, armies may assemble, calumny may defame, but the truth of God will go forth boldly, nobly, and independent till it has penetrated every continent, visited every clime, swept every country, and sounded in every ear, till the purposes of God shall be accomplished and the great Jehovah shall say the work is done.

1. We believe in God, the Eternal Father, and in His Son, Jesus Christ, and in the Holy Ghost.
2. We believe that men will be punished for their own sins, and not for Adam's transgression.

3. We believe that through the atonement, all mankind may be saved, by obedience to the laws and ordinances of the Gospel.

4. We believe that the first principles and ordinances of the Gospel are: first, Faith in the Lord Jesus Christ; second, Repentance; third, Baptism by immersion for the remission of sins; fourth, Laying on of hands for the gift of the Holy Ghost.

5. We believe that a man must be called of God, by prophecy, and by the laying on of hands by those who are in authority, to preach the Gospel and administer in the ordinances thereof.

6. We believe in the same organization that existed in the Primitive Church, namely, apostles, prophets, pastors, teachers, evangelists, and so forth.

7. We believe in the gift of tongues, prophecy, revelation, visions, healing, interpretation of tongues, and so forth.

8. We believe the Bible to be the word of God as far as it is translated correctly; we also believe the Book of Mormon to be the word of God.

9. We believe all that God has revealed, all that He does now reveal, and we believe that He will yet reveal many great and important things pertaining to the Kingdom of God.

10. We believe in the literal gathering of Israel and in the restoration of the Ten Tribes; that Zion (the New

Jerusalem) will be built upon the American continent; that Christ will reign personally upon the earth; and, that the earth will be renewed and receive its paradisiacal glory.

11. We claim the privilege of worshiping Almighty God according to the dictates of our own conscience, and allow all men the same privilege, let them worship how, where, or what they may.

12. We believe in being subject to kings, presidents, rulers, and magistrates, in obeying, honoring, and sustaining the law.

13. We believe in being honest, true, chaste, benevolent, virtuous, and in doing good to all men; indeed, we may say that we follow the admonition of Paul—We believe all things, we hope all things, we have endured many things, and hope to be able to endure all things. If there is anything virtuous, lovely, or of good report or praiseworthy, we seek after these things.

Surprising Quotes from Mormon Leaders

Joseph Smith Predicts the Civil War—in 1832!

"Verily, thus saith the Lord concerning the wars that will shortly come to pass, beginning at the rebellion of South Carolina, which will eventually terminate in the death and misery of many souls; and the time will come that war will be poured out upon all nations, beginning at this place. For behold, the Southern States shall be divided against the Northern States, and the Southern States will call on other nations, even the nation of Great Britain, as it is called, and they shall also call upon other nations, in order to defend themselves against other nations; and then war shall be poured out upon all nations. And it shall come to pass, after many days, slaves shall rise up against their masters, who shall be marshaled and disciplined for war." —Joseph Smith, *Doctrines and Covenants* 87:1–4

Joseph Smith Is Like God—or Else!

"God made Aaron to be the mouthpiece for the children of Israel and He will make me to be a God to you in His stead, and the Elders to be mouth for me, and if you don't like it, you must lump it." —Joseph Smith, *History of the Church* 6:319–20

Joseph Smith Is Like Muhammad

"I will be to this generation a second Muhammed, whose motto in treating for peace was 'the Alcoran [Qur'an] or the sword.' So shall it eventually be with us, 'Joseph Smith or the sword!'"[1] —Joseph Smith

No Wine, Liquor, Tobacco, Coffee, or Tea

"Word of Wisdom . . . That inasmuch as any man drinketh wine or strong drink among you, behold it is not good, neither meet in the sight of your Father . . . strong drinks are not for the belly but for the washing of your bodies . . . and again, tobacco is not for the body, neither for the belly, and is not good for man . . . and again, hot drinks are not for the body or belly."[2] —Joseph Smith, *Doctrine and Covenants* 89:1–9

Brigham Young's Teaching Is Scripture

"In my doctrinal teachings I have taught many things not written in any book, ancient or modern, and yet notwithstanding the many things I have told the people, I have never looked into the Bible, Book of Mormon or the Doctrine and Covenants, or any of our church works to see whether they agreed with them or not. When I have spoken by the power of God and the Holy Ghost, it is truth, it is Scripture, and I have no fears but that it will agree with all that has been revealed in every particular." —Brigham Young, *Deseret News*, June 6, 1877

Brigham Young Uninterested in Revelations

"I am not a visionary man, neither am I given to prophesying. When I want any of that done I call on Brother Heber—he is my prophet. He loves to prophesy, and I love to hear him. I scarcely ever say much about revelations or visions." —Brigham Young, *Journal of Discourses* 1:132:33

Joseph Smith: "I am not so much a Christian"

"I am not so much a 'Christian' as men suppose I am. When a man undertakes to ride me for a horse, I feel disposed to kick up and throw him off, and ride him." —Joseph Smith, *History of the Church* 5:335

Monogamy a Roman Deception

"Since the founding of the Roman Empire monogamy has prevailed more extensively than in times previous to that. The founders of that ancient empire were robbers and women stealers, and made laws favoring monogamy in consequence of the scarcity of women among them and hence this monogamic system which now prevails throughout Christendom, and which had been so fruitful a source of prostitution and whoredom through all the Christian monogamic cities of the Old and New World, until rottenness and decay are at the root of their institutions both national and religious." —Brigham Young, *Journal of Discourses* 11:128

Why Some Men Go on Missions

"We have at times sent men on missions to get rid of them; but they have generally come back. Some think it is an imposition upon the world to send such men among them. But which is best—to keep them here to pollute others, or to send them where pollution is more prevalent? . . . We have tried to turn the filthy ones out of the flock, but they will not always stay out." —Brigham Young, *Journal of Discourses* 7:7:228–29

Mormons to Save America

"Will the Constitution be destroyed? No: it will be held inviolate by this people; and, as Joseph Smith said, 'The time will come when the destiny of the nation will hang upon a single thread. At that critical juncture, this people will step forth and save it from the threatened destruction.' It will be so." — Brigham Young, *Journal of Discourses* 7:15

Jews Can't Be Christians

"Can you make a Christian of Jew? I tell you, nay. If a Jew comes into this Church, and honestly professes to be a Saint, a follower of Christ, and if the blood of Judah is in his veins, he will apostatize. He may have been born and bred a Jew, have the face of a Jew, speak the language of the Jews . . . and have openly professed to be a Jew all his days; but I will tell you a secret—there is not a particle of the blood of Judaism in him, if he has become a true Christian, a Saint of God; for if there is, he will most assuredly leave the Church of Christ, or that blood will be purged out of his veins." —Brigham Young, *Journal of Discourses* 2:142

Non-Mormons Are Anti-Christ

"Every spirit that confesses that Joseph Smith is a prophet, that he lived and died a prophet, and that the Book of Mormon is true, is of God, and every spirit that does not is of Anti-Christ." —Brigham Young, LDS Conference at Nauvoo, October 1844

LDS President Commissioned by the American Founding Fathers

"Every one of those men that signed the Declaration of Independence with General Washington called upon me as an Apostle of the Lord Jesus Christ, in the Temple at St. George, two consecutive nights, and demanded at my hands that I should go forth and attend to the ordinances of the House of God for them." —Wilford Woodruff, *Conference Report*, April 10, 1898

Noah's Ark Built on Atlantic Coast

"According to the words of the Prophet Joseph, mankind in that age continued to emigrate eastwardly until they reached the country on or near the Atlantic coast; and that in or near Carolina, Noah built his remarkable ship, in which he, his family, and all kinds of animals lived a few days over one year without coming out of it." —Oliver B. Huntington, *The Juvenile Instructor*, November 15, 1895

On Birth Control

"Birth Control leads to damnation." —Joseph Field Smith, *Doctrines of Salvation*, vol. 2, 89

Metals Grow

"Gold and silver grow, and so does every other kind of metal, the same as the hair upon my head, or the wheat in the field; they do not grow as fast, but they are all the time composing or decomposing." —Brigham Young, *Journal of Discourses* 1:219

What Joseph Smith Knows

"No man can learn you more than what I told you. . . . I have an old book of the New Testament in Hebrew, Latin, German and Greek. I have been reading the German and find it to be the most correct. . . . I know more than all the world put together. . . . I have now preached a little Latin, a little Hebrew, Greek and German, and I have fulfilled all. I am not so big a fool as many have taken me to be. The Germans know that I read German correct." —Joseph Smith, *Times and Seasons*, vol. 5, 614–17

Joseph Smith Was a Lawyer

"I am a lawyer; I am a big lawyer and comprehend heaven, earth and hell, to bring forth knowledge that shall cover up all lawyers, doctors and other big goodies." —Joseph Smith, *History of the Church* 5:289

Mormons as Mean as Devils

"I have many a time in this stand, dared the world to produce as mean devils as we can; we can beat them at anything. We have the greatest and smoothest liars in the world, the cunningest and most adroit thieves, and any other shade of character that you can mention. We can pick out Elders in Israel right here who can beat the world at gambling . . . I can produce Elders here who can shave their smartest shavers, and take their money from them. We can beat the world at any game." —Brigham Young, *Journal of Discourses* 4:77

The Unknown Joseph Smith

"You don't know me; you never knew my heart. No man knows my history. I cannot tell it; I shall never undertake. I don't blame anyone for not believing my history. If I had not experienced what I have, I could not have believed it myself." — Joseph Smith, *Journal of Discourses* 6:11

Notes

Prologue: Scenes from the Land of the Saints

1. Walter Kirn, "Mormons Rock," *Newsweek*, June 11, 2011, http://www.thedailybeast.com/newsweek/2011/06/05/mormons-rock.html.

2. Every vignette in this book is based on actual events either observed by the author or recounted to the author by those involved. Names have in almost all cases been altered and locations in some cases have. This was either at the request of those involved or, in one or two cases, to comply with concerns of military security. The views expressed in these vignettes are not necessarily those of the author or his publisher but are rather intended to illustrate the many facets of opinion that surround modern Mormonism.

Introduction: Engine of the Mormon Ascent

1. Wallace Stegner, *Mormon Country* (Lincoln: University of Nebraska Press, 2003), 47.

2. The Church's official statistics are regularly reported on the LDS Newsroom website at www.mormonnewsroom.org.

3. Rodney Stark, *The Rise of Mormonism*, ed. Reid L. Neilson (New York: Columbia University Press, 2005), 22.

4. "Mormon Church's Public Relations Effort amid Olympics Games Sparks Debate," *Salt Lake Tribune*, March 19, 2001, http://business.highbeam.com/3563/article-1G1-71876499/mormon-church-public-relations-effort-amid-olympics.

5. *Doctrine and Covenants*, 130:18–19.

6. Ibid., 101:80.

7. Leonard J. Arrington, Feramorz Y. Fox, and Dean L. May, *Building the City of God: Community & Cooperation Among the Mormons* (Chicago: University of Illinois Press, 1992), 15.

8. Chris Lehmann, "Pennies from Heaven: How Mormon Economics Shape the GOP," *Harper's Magazine*, October 2011.

9. Ibid.

Chapter 1: The Mormon View of Mormonism

1. Michael Ruse, "Voting for a Mormon," *Chronicle of Higher Education*, November 30, 2011.

2. Kathryn Flake, interview for "The Mormons," *Frontline* and *American Experience* co-production, prod. Helen Whitney, April 30 and May 1, 2007.

Chapter 2: In Search of True Religion

1. Joseph Field Smith, *Doctrines of Salvation*, ed. Bruce R. McConkie, vol. 1 (Salt Lake City: Bookcraft, 1956), 188–89.

2. Robert Remini, *Joseph Smith* (New York: Viking Penguin, 2002), 11.

3. Ibid., 16.

4. "Money Diggers," *Palmyra Herald*, July 24, 1822, quoted in Robert Remini, *Joseph Smith* (New York: Viking Penguin, 2002), 16–17.

5. Lucy Mack Smith, *History of Joseph Smith by His Mother* (Salt Lake City: Deseret Book, 1853), 62.

Chapter 3: Joseph Smith: Prophet and Magician

1. Marvin S. Hill, review of *Joseph Smith's New York Reputation Reexamined*, by Rodger I. Anderson, *BYU Studies* 30, no. 3 (Fall 1990), quoted in Michael Quinn, *Early Mormonism and the Magic World View* (Salt Lake City: Signature Books, 1998), 59.

2. Richard Lyman Bushman, *Joseph Smith: Rough Stone Rolling* (New York: Alfred A. Knopf, 2005), 55.

3. Ibid., 38.

4. Lucy Mack Smith, *History of Joseph Smith*, 74.

5. This account of the appearance of Moroni is from the official LDS version found in *Pearl of Great Price*.

6. This account of the fourth appearance of Moroni is from Lucy Mack Smith's *History of Joseph Smith by His Mother*. It differs slightly from the official version in *Pearl of Great Price*.

7. Remini, *Joseph Smith*, 49.

8. Michael Quinn, *Early Mormonism and the Magic World View* (Salt Lake City: Signature Books, 1998), 26–27.

9. Bushman, *Rough Stone*, 50.

10. Quinn, *Early Mormonism*, quoted in Mitch Horowitz, *Occult America: White House Séances, Ouija Circles, Masons, and the Secret Mystic History of Our Nation* (New York: Bantam Books, 2009), 23.

11. Glen Leonard (former director, Latter-day Saints Church History Museum), in discussion with the author, January 31, 2012.

12. Remini, *Joseph Smith*, 50.

Chapter 4: The Golden Plates

1. Orson Pratt, *Divine Authenticity of the Book of Mormon*, (Liverpool: F. D. Richards, 1850), 1–2.

2. Emma Smith Bidamon, *Notes of Interview with Joseph Smith, III*, 1879, quoted in Bushman, *Rough Stone*, 57.

3. Fawn M. Brodie, *No Man Knows My History: The Life of Joseph Smith* (New York: Vintage Books, 1945), 61.

4. Pratt, *Divine Authenticity*, 1–2.

5. Isaac Hale, in an affidavit given 20 March, 1834, and reported in the *Susquehanna Register* (Montrose, Pennsylvania), May 1, 1834, quoted in Brodie, *No Man Knows*, 440.

6. Brodie, *No Man Knows*, 37.

7. Ibid.

8. Ibid., 38.

9. Joseph Smith, *History of the Church of Jesus Christ of Latter-day Saints*, ed. B. H. Roberts, 2nd ed. rev. (Salt Lake City: Deseret News, 1957),1:54–55.

10. Brodie, *No Man Knows*, 79–80.

11. Royal Skousen, ed., *The Book of Mormon: The Earliest Text* (New Haven, CT: Yale University Press, 2009), 737.

12. Ibid., 738.

13. Of "The Three Witnesses" who attested to the existence of the golden plates, all eventually left the Church. Of "The Eight Witnesses" who also said they saw the plates, two died early, one left the church never to return and two left for a season but returned eventually. Only three stayed true to the end and all of these were Smith family members.

14. *Book of Commandments*, 16:13–37.

Chapter 5: An American Gospel

1. Joseph Smith, *History of the Church*, 4:461.

2. Brodie, *No Man Knows*, 62.

3. Jacob 7:26 (Book of Mormon).

4. Mark Twain's cutting analysis of the Book of Mormon is found in his travelogue *Roughing It*, first published in 1872.

5. Brodie, *No Man Knows*, 54.

6. Ibid., 70.

7. Ibid., 69.

8. *Wayne Sentinel*, June 1, 1827, quoted in Brodie, *No Man Knows*, 50.

9. Brodie, *No Man Knows*, 46.

10. Ethan Smith, *View of the Hebrews; or, The Tribes of Israel in America*, 2nd ed. (Poultney, VT, 1825), 184, quoted in Brodie, *No Man Knows*, 46.

11. Smith, *View of the Hebrews*, 223, quoted in Brodie, *No Man Knows*, 46–47.

12. Brodie, *No Man Knows*, 47.

13. For these affidavits and additional discussion of Solomon Spaulding's *Manuscript Found*, see Appendix B in Fawn Brodie's *No Man Knows My History*, 442–56.

14. Quoted in Richard Ostling and Joan K. Ostling, *Mormon America: The Power and the Promise* (New York: HarperCollins, 2007), 163.

15. Ibid., 276.

Chapter 6: A New Breed of Men

1. Parley P. Pratt, *Key to the Science of Theology* (Liverpool: F. D. Richards, 1855), 66.

2. This account appeared in the *Latter-Day Saints Messenger and Advocate*, Kirtland, Ohio, October 1834. It is quoted by Lucy Mack Smith in her history and is reprinted in *Pearl of Great Price*.

3. Remini, *Joseph Smith*, 100.

4. *Doctrine and Covenants*, Section 38.

5. Most scholars, including esteemed LDS historian Richard Bushman, conclude that Joseph Smith had between twenty-eight and thirty-three wives, that ten of these were under the age of twenty and that another ten were already married when they married Smith. The youngest was fourteen. Historian M. Fawn Brodie argued that there is evidence for forty-eight wives in her controversial biography, *No Man Knows My History: The Life of Joseph Smith*.

6. *Doctrine and Covenants*, 132:58–62

7. Brodie, *No Man Knows*, 89.

Chapter 7: Among a Progressing People

1. Heber Kimball, sermon delivered on September 28, 1856. *Journal of Discourses*, 4:108.

2. A legacy of duplicity over polygamy lived on in the Church. For example, Joseph F. Smith, the Prophet's nephew, issued his "Second Manifesto" against polygamy in 1904 and yet approved plural marriages in 1906 and 1907.

3. *Journal of Discourses*, 4:78.

Chapter 8: The Earthly Fruit of Faith

1. *Journal of Discourses*, 9:157.

2. Harold Schindler, "Conan Doyle's Tale of Mormonism Had Utah Faithful Seeing Scarlet," *Salt Lake Tribune*, April 10, 1994, D1.

Chapter 9: The Work Unfinished

1. Joseph Smith, *History of the Church*, 6:408–409

2. "Public Expresses Mixed Views of Islam, Mormonism," Pew Forum on Religion and Public Life, September 26, 2007, http://www.pewforum.org/Public-Expresses-Mixed-Views-of-Islam-Mormonism.aspx.

3. Kirn, "Mormons Rock."

Appendix B: Surprising Quotes from Mormon Leaders

1. Brodie, *No Man Knows*, 230–31.

2. The Church later ruled that "hot drinks" referred to coffee and tea. Even later, caffeinated drinks were included in the ban.

Bibliography

Arrington, Leonard J., Feramorz Y. Fox, and Deal L. May. *Building the City of God: Community and Cooperation Among the Mormons*. Chicago: University of Illinois Press, 1992.

Bagley, Will. *Brigham Young and the Massacre at Mountain Meadows*. Norman, OK: University of Oklahoma Press, 2002.

Batchelor, Mary, Marianne Watson, and Anne Wilde. *Voices in Harmony: Contemporary Women Celebrate Plural Marriage*. Salt Lake City: Principle Voices, 2000.

Beckwith, Francis J., Carl Mosser, and Paul Owen, eds. *The New Mormon Challenge*. Grand Rapids: Zondervan, 2002.

Benedict, Jeff. *The Mormon Way of Doing Business*. New York: Hachette, 2007.

Berner, Brad K. *Unsaintly Saints: The Mormons in Their Own Words*. Moscow, Russia: Brad K. Berner, 2008.

Bringhurst, Newel G. *Brigham Young and the Expanding American Frontier*. Boston: Little, Brown, 1986.

Brodie, Fawn M. *No Man Knows My History: The Life of Joseph Smith*. New York: Vintage Books, 1945.

Bushman, Richard Lyman. *Joseph Smith: Rough Stone Rolling*. New York, Vantage Books, 2005.

Cowdrey, Wayne L., Howard A. Davis, and Arthur Vanick. *Who Really Wrote the Book of Mormon?* St. Louis: Concordia, 2001.

Flake, Kathleen. *The Politics of American Religious Identity: The Seating of Reed Smoot, Mormon Apostle*. Chapel Hill: University of North Carolina Press, 2004.

Givens, Terryl L. *By the Hand of Mormon: The American Scripture That Launched a New World Religion*. Oxford: Oxford University Press, 2002.

———*A People of Paradox: A History of Mormon Culture*. Oxford: Oxford University Press, 2007.

Hatch, Nathan O. *The Democratization of American Christianity*. New Haven, CT: Yale University Press, 1989.

Horowitz, Mitch. *Occult America: White House Séances, Ouija Circles, Masons, and the Secret Mystic History of Our Nation*. New York: Bantam Books, 2009.

Jackson, Andrew. *Mormonism Explained: What Latter-day Saints Teach and Practice*. Wheaton, IL: Crossway Books, 2008.

Jessop, Carolyn. *Escape*. With Laura Palmer. New York: Broadway Books, 2007.

Krakauer, Jon. *Under the Banner of Heaven*. With Laura Palmer. New York: Anchor Books, 2004.

Mauss, Armand. *The Angel and the Beehive: The Mormon Struggle with Assimilation*. Chicago: The University of Chicago Press, 1989.

Millet, Robert L. *The Mormon Faith: A New Look at Christianity*. Salt Lake City: Shadow Mountain, 1998.

O'Dea, Thomas. *The Mormons*. Chicago: University of Chicago Press, 1957.

Ostling, Richard, and Joan K. Ostling. *Mormon America*. New York: Harper Collins, 2007.

Palmer, Grant H. *An Insider's View of Mormon Origins*. Salt Lake City: Signature Books, 2002.

Putnam, Robert D., and David E. Campbell. *American Grace: How Religion Divides and Unites Us*. New York: Simon & Schuster, 2010.

Quinn, D. Michael. *Early Mormonism and the Magic World View*. Salt Lake City: Signature Books, 1998.

———*Same-Sex Dynamics Among Nineteenth-Century Americans: A Mormon Example*. Chicago: University of Illinois Press, 1996.

Riess, Jana, and Christopher Kimball. *Mormonism for Dummies*. Hoboken: Wiley, 2005.

Remini, Robert V. *Joseph Smith: A Penguin Life*. New York: Viking Books, 2002.

Roberts, David. *Devil's Gate: Brigham Young and the Great Mormon Handcart Tragedy*. New York: Simon & Schuster, 2008.

Shipps, Jan. *Mormonism: The Story of a New Religious Tradition*. Chicago: University of Illinois Press, 1987.

Skousen, Royal, ed. *The Book of Mormon: The Earliest Text*. New Haven, CT: Yale University Press, 2009.

Smith, James R. *Mormon Mission Prep: A Practical Guide to Spiritual and Physical Preparation*. Lehi, UT: Simply Fresh Designs, 2011.

Stegner, Wallace. *Mormon Country*. Lincoln, NE: Bison Books, 2003.

———*The Gathering of Zion: The Story of the Mormon Trail*. New York: McGraw-Hill Book Company, 1964.

Walker, Ronald, David B. Whittaker, and James B. Allen. *Mormon History*. Chicago: University of Illinois Press, 2001.

Stephen Mansfield is a writer and speaker best known for his groundbreaking books on the role of religion in history, leadership, and politics. He first came to international attention with *The Faith of George W. Bush*, the *New York Times* best seller that influenced Oliver Stone's film *W.* His book on *The Faith of Barack Obama* was another international bestseller. He has written celebrated biographies of Booker T. Washington, George Whitefield, Winston Churchill, and Abraham Lincoln, among others. Known for aggressively researching his books, Mansfield worked in a brewery while writing *The Search for God and Guinness* and was embedded with US troops in Iraq for his study of faith among America's warriors.

Stephen speaks around the world on topics of faith, leadership, and culture. He is also the founder of two firms, The Mansfield Group (MansfieldGroup.com) and Chartwell Literary Group (ChartwellLiterary.com). He is a frequent commentator on television news programs and an outspoken advocate for a variety of social causes. A single sentence from one of his books about faith in the Oval Office captures the central belief of his work: "If a man's faith is sincere, it is the most important thing about him and it is impossible to understand who he is and how he will lead without first understanding the religious vision that informs his life."

Mansfield lives in Nashville and Washington, DC with his wife, Beverly, who is an award-winning songwriter and producer. For further information, log onto MansfieldGroup.com.

IF YOU ENJOYED THIS BOOK, WILL YOU CONSIDER SHARING THE MESSAGE WITH OTHERS?

Mention the book in a blog post or through Facebook, Twitter, Pinterest, or upload a picture through Instagram.

Recommend this book to those in your small group, book club, workplace, and classes.

Head over to facebook.com/worthypublishing, "LIKE" the page, and post a comment as to what you enjoyed the most.

Tweet "I recommend reading #themormonizingofamerica by @MansfieldWrites // @worthypub"

Pick up a copy for someone you know who would be challenged and encouraged by this message.

Write a book review online.

Visit us at worthypublishing.com

twitter.com/worthypub

facebook.com/worthypublishing

instagram.com/worthypub

youtube.com/worthypublishing

CPSIA information can be obtained
at www.ICGtesting.com
Printed in the USA
BVHW041423300720
585048BV00011B/67

9 781683 972884